MUSIC AND
MATHEMATICS

MUSIC AND MATHEMATICS

Canon D.B. Eperson

The Book Guild Ltd
Sussex, England

First published in Great Britain in 2002 by
The Book Guild Ltd
25 High Street,
Lewes, East Sussex
BN7 2LU

Copyright © Canon D.B. Eperson, 2002

The right of Canon D.B. Eperson to be identified as the author of
this work has been asserted by him in accordance with the
Copyright, Designs and Patents Act 1988.

All rights reserved. No part of this publication may be
reproduced, transmitted, or stored in a retrieval system, in any form
or by any means, without permission in writing from the publisher,
nor be otherwise circulated in any form of binding or cover other
than that in which it is published and without a similar condition
being imposed on the subsequent purchaser.

Typesetting in Times by
Keyboard Services, Luton, Bedfordshire

Printed in Great Britain by
Bookcraft (Bath) Ltd, Avon

A catalogue record for this book is available from
The British Library

ISBN 1 85776 636 9

CONTENTS

1	Childhood and Schooldays	1
2	My Musical Education	8
3	Christ Church, Oxford	11
4	Sherborne School	18
5	Educating a Mathematical Genius: Alan Turing at Sherborne School	27
6	Leisure-Time Activities	33
7	Charminster	49
8	Chichester	67
9	Canterbury	81
10	Worthing	97

v

1

Childhood and Schooldays

I was fortunate in having a happy childhood in a home provided by my parents, who lived harmoniously together throughout their married lives. My mother, Anne Jessop Birkby, was the daughter of a Bradford wool merchant. She was at St Katharine's College, in North London, when she met my father, Joseph William Eperson, who was at Westminster College; they were both training to be teachers. I was fortunate in inheriting their musical talents: I still have the volume of Mozart's piano sonatas presented to my mother for being the organist at her college, whilst my father was a singer and a violinist, I remember that he made a one-stringed violin out of a cigar box for amusement.

They continued teaching whilst my sister and I were babies – my mother as a lecturer in domestic science at Battersea Polytechnic, and my father at a boys' school under the LCC (London County Council), and after World War I at a day continuation school. After we moved from Turnham Green to East Acton he had an illness that resulted in his being classified as C3 when examined for military service, and he spent some years travelling daily to Ilford to work in a factory making shells.

At our new four-bedroomed house, The Haven, 48 Perryn Road, East Acton, there was a large back garden, half of which was a croquet lawn bordered by flower beds, and the other half was used for growing fruit and vegetables. My father was a keen gardener, and did some experimental work on growing potatoes, for which he was rewarded by Dobbies, the Scottish seedsmen, with a gold medal. The results were published in a booklet, price 1d. He also cultivated a 10-rod allotment, on which he erected a wooden shed that he had constructed. He was an excellent draughtsman and carpenter, and later on he drew the builder's plans for our new house on Torbay.

My sister Doreen was born in 1905, a year after me. I have many photographs of her as a bonny babe. We were happy companions in our young days; at home and on holidays in Upper or Lower Brixham, and our chief pastimes were croquet and french cricket.

When we went to Brixham, we always went by train from Paddington, when the first excitement was the stop at Taunton, where a second engine helped the train up the incline en route for Exeter. It was uncoupled at the top of the incline, and the train rattled at great speed downhill. The next thrill was the sea-side track through Dawlish, with tunnels through the red sandstone cliffs to Teignmouth. On arrival at Churston station a horse-drawn cab took us to Hillside, Dashpers, Higher Brixham, where we lodged with Mr and Mrs George Matthews, carpenter and undertaker. Although I have had few train journeys, I still retain my interest in trains and railway tracks.

When I was nine years old, I attended the junior department at the Acton Central School, and had the good fortune to win a £100 scholarship, which covered the fees for two years at Colet Court Preparatory School and my first two years at St Paul's School. It soon became evident that I had inherited from my parents the greatest possible gift, as the weekly reports that I took home to be signed by my parents almost invariably showed that I was top in all subjects, except drawing, in which I was usually amongst the top five out of twenty boys. Any success that I have ever enjoyed in my lifetime I owe to my parents, and I feel great gratitude to them. The only credit I can claim is that I did work conscientiously; I recollect that on one birthday I took so long over my homework that the ice cream, which my parents had obtained as a celebration, had melted by the time I finished. But then, I realise that the trait of persistence was another gift inherited from my parents.

Each schoolday I travelled to Hammersmith Broadway by tram – fare $\frac{1}{2}$d – and although I was never top of the class at St Paul's School, I won a classical scholarship and slowly climbed up the classical side until I reached the lower eighth, my chief pleasure being writing Latin and Greek verse.

During my first year as a 12-year-old new boy in 1916 an event occurred that virtually decided my main future occupation as an adult: I attended an after-school lantern lecture on astronomy, and was so fascinated by the pictures that I borrowed from the school library every book on the subject.

Many years later I bought a huge book on astronomy (I forget the author's name), and Sir James Hopwood Jean's book, *The Stars in their Courses* (1931). Little did I dream then that one day I should be giving a series of Christmastide lectures on astronomy to children at the Science Museum, London, showing the slides used by the professional lecturer who was on sick leave.

In 1509 Dean Colet had founded St Paul's School for the free education in 'Laten and Greke' of 153 boys. I was fortunate to be one of their twentieth-century successors, but my classical education terminated somewhat abruptly when a small group of boys was engaged upon translating Thucydides' history of the Persian Wars, which contained an account of the postponement of a battle because of an eclipse of the moon. The form-master commented that they would have been especially alarmed as it was a full moon that was eclipsed. Up went my hand. 'Please, sir, you can't have an eclipse of the moon unless it is full.' I was invited to explain why this was so.

I drew diagrams on the blackboard showing the alignment of the sun, moon and the earth during an eclipse; a few days later I was transferred to the mathematical eighth form, where a few boys were studying to obtain university scholarships in mathematics, and others were hoping to become actuaries, etc.

My mathematical education at Colet Court had not been enjoyable: it was based upon Pendlebury's *Arithmetic*, Dalton's *Algebra*, and Hall and Stevens' *School Geometry* – a watered-down version of the book that my father had studied when at college. Homework often consisted of memorising the congruence theorems and the *pons asinorum* of *Euclid Book 1*. But his axioms, definitions and postulates were beyond my comprehension. I appreciated the wider syllabus of mathematics on the classical side of St Paul's School, which included trigonometry and Godfrey and Siddon's *Algebra*, and eventually reached arithmetic and geometric progressions, and the ingenious method of 'proof by induction', which aroused my enthusiasm for the subject.

Captain H.R. Pullinger was in charge of the mathematical eighth and of mathematical education of the 'army class', which occasionally occupied the front rows of the classroom, whilst we mathematicians sat in the back row in order of seniority, the oldest being near the window. At first I worked on my own, but soon was joined by three younger boys – J.C.P. Miller, F.S. Hadland and H.E. Carpenter – whilst my seniors were W.G.N. Lightfoot and G.W. Furlonge. The books we used were Smith's *Treatise on Algebra*, Smith's *Conic Sections*, Loney's *Trigonometry* and his *Statics and Dynamics*, Durell's *Plane Geometry Part II* and later on his *Modern Geometry*, Askwith's *Analytical Geometry*, Edwards' *Differential and Integral Calculus*. There was a large bookcase full of mathematical publications, the most popular of which was Rouse-Ball's *Mathematical Recreations and Essays*. I remember our being amused when 'Pully' announced that at last he had been able to acquire a 'second-hand Salmon'. We worked out selected examples from these textbooks, and only went to Pully for help when we were in difficulty. We were expected to do at least two hours of homework each weekday evening.

4

I was intrigued by Pascal's Theorem and its dual, Brianchon's Theorem, and spent some time during a summer holiday trying to find elementary geometrical theorems that had a dual – interchanging the words 'line' and 'point', 'concurrent' and 'collinear', etc.

In the year 1922–3 I was the only boy studying for a university scholarship, and working on old Cambridge examination papers: I was duly entered to sit for the 'Emmanuel' group of colleges – usually thought to be easier than the 'Trinity' group. But Pully discovered that in the week before the Cambridge examination there was a scholarship examination at Oxford, and he recommended me to enter as a trial run in order to gain experience of a university examination. There were five scholarships worth £80 per annum on offer, and one was invited on the entrance form to express an order of preference: I placed Christ Church as my No. 5, as I had been told that it was the most expensive Oxford college. I thoroughly enjoyed my few days living in 'digs', and I quite liked doing the papers, especially the one on general knowledge, where my knowledge of Gilbert and Sullivan operas came in useful, and my essay was lighthearted. I was very impressed by the architecture of the Oxford colleges and university buildings – I had had an enjoyable holiday!

A few days later I was at Emmanuel College, Cambridge, and had written two papers, when I received a telegram offering me the Christ Church scholarship, which I readily accepted. I had not enjoyed the Cambridge examination papers, which were of a different kind from those at Oxford. This was a tremendous stroke of good fortune. My parents naturally were delighted, and the school honoured me by appointing me as one of the small group of prefects. I was but one of the 32 boys who obtained university scholarships or exhibitions that year, four of which were at Christ Church – two classics, one science and myself.

World War I was still raging when I became old enough to

join the ranks of the officers training corps, and attended camps during the summer vacations at Strensall, Yorkshire, and at Mychett on Salisbury Plain, besides shooting on the firing ranges at Bisley. When I returned to school in 1922 for my last year, I was the only surviving NCO, and so became the company sergeant major of the school OTC. I probably increased my lung power through calling the troops to attention on the parade ground for the weekly drill.

Each Wednesday afternoon was devoted to sport – cricket in the summer term, and rugger in the other two terms: we had to travel to the playing fields within sight of Wormwood Scrubbs prison. I did not shine in either of these activities, but I enjoyed playing chess, for which I gained two prizes. Only once did I join the school team, playing against another London school, when my young opponent castled on the king's side, and allowed me to mate his king at once. When Sir George Thomas, the national chess champion, came to the school to play simultaneously against about 20 boys playing black, I was one of the few boys that defeated him.

The last day of my seven years at the school arrived – Apposition Day, 1923, when speeches were made, prizes distributed and some athletic sports held on the adjoining playing field. I joined in the Old Pauline Handicap Race, and was given about 50 yards' start in a 200-yard race by the handicapper – the head prefect – who intended to insult me by putting me in the same category as the older and more corpulent Old Paulines, but I was first past the post, and won a small silver cup, awarded by Mappin and Webb. When I arrived home, I found our house had been burgled in the absence of the rest of the family, who had gone on holiday to Jersey by day, and I was to follow by the night boat from Southampton. Apparently the burglar had been disturbed and fled, leaving some mats in the front garden. The train from Waterloo was packed and I travelled in the corridor, and a cold night on the deck of the boat followed. I met my family on arrival next morning at St Helier, and we went on to a nearby beach, where I promptly fell asleep.

I had kept a daily diary whilst at school, but I find hardly any reference to school events in them, as they deal with home affairs, and so form the basis of the next chapter.

2

My Musical Education

We lived within a stone's throw of St Dunstan's Church, East Acton, which in pre-World War I days was filled every Sunday with a large congregation of adults and children. There was a semi-professional choir, consisting of 12 tenors and basses, 2 lady contraltos (unrobed and seated behind the choir stalls) and 24 boy trebles, whom I joined at nine years of age, after a brief period as a probationer. We were paid 1d for attendance at each choir practice, on Mondays and Tuesdays for boys only, and a full choir practice on Friday nights, and 2s 6d every three months for singing at the Sunday services. We were not taught how to read, and for many years I sang 'by ear'. We used the words of the *Old Cathedral Psalter*, together with a large manuscript book of Anglican chants, and the standard edition of *Hymns Ancient and Modern* (which I still possess). The canticles were usually sung to settings by Victorian composers, and we had a small repertoire of simple anthems. The highlight of each year was the performance of Stainer's *Crucifixion* with the aid of tenor and bass soloists from St Paul's Cathedral.

I can clearly recall the Sunday morning when the service was interrupted by protesting suffragettes, whose cries were promptly drowned by a fortissimo outburst from the organ, played by Mr Doe. Another memorable incident occurred during the war, when the choir practice was halted by a nearby anti-aircraft gun firing 101 consecutive salvoes; Zeppelin air raids on London were frequent. I greatly enjoyed the choir practices and the Sunday services conducted by the vicar, the Revd W. le Patourel, who acted as choirmaster until he volunteered to be a naval chaplain. In the boys' vestry there was hung a letter from him to his 'dear boys', written from HMS *Defence* just before he lost his life at the Battle of Jutland. The curate, the Revd B. Boustead, conducted the services, until a new vicar was appointed – the Revd H.M.M. Bevan.

In course of time I became the head choirboy, but I can recollect singing only one solo – the first verse of Atwood's *Come, Holy Ghost*. When I lost the top register of my treble voice, I sang the alto part for a year, sitting alongside the choirmen. I took the trouble of copying out the alto part of the Anglican chants in the mss book, which I think was an amalgam of chants by well-known Victorian composers from published collections.

Every Sunday evening our family made music together: my mother accompanied on the piano the songs and hymns sung by my sister Doreen and myself, and my father would play the violin or join in the singing. After the war we all went to the Princes' Theatre in London on Saturday evenings to hear Gilbert and Sullivan operas: the first one I heard was *The Yeomen of the Guard*, and I was reduced to tears by the finale, when Jack Point sang 'I have a song to sing-o'. It was not long before we had seen all the current productions from the theatre gallery, for which we had queued up all the afternoon so as to get the best seats there. We had a vocal score of the *Mikado*, and we soon added all its melodies to our repertoire. I was much older when I first went on my own to the Old Vic or Sadler's Wells, and gradually increased my acquaintance with operas by Wagner, Mozart, Strauss and Vaughan Williams. My mother's favourite composer was Mendelssohn, and she frequently played some of his *Songs without words*, but after Doreen and I had left home, she and my father had no further opportunity for using their musical talents.

When at school I usually got home first about 5.30 p.m. – Doreen went to Chiswick High School for Girls – and had an hour or so to myself: for several years I used this time to learn how to play the piano by picking out hymn tunes, but without acquiring any playing technique. Ultimately I could play the four-part harmony of hymn tunes, and even attempted to play the slow movements of piano sonatas by Mozart and Beethoven at a funereal pace. For the entertainment of guests at my twenty-first birthday party in 1925 I compiled an 'operetta' entitled *Dope*, selecting some of Gilbert's *Bab Ballads* and setting them to music, and writing lyrics that fitted tunes from the Savoy operas. It was performed by three baritones – my father, a friend from the church choir, and myself – with my mother providing the piano accompaniment. It received only one performance – a world record?

As I grew older the range of my voice increased, and I spent most of my life singing tenor parts, until in old age I reverted to being a bass in groups of unaccompanied singers.

3

Christ Church, Oxford

As a twenty-first birthday present my school friend A.A.W. Gray gave me a framed 1673 print of Christ Church, Oxford – made by Loggan in the days before Sir Christopher Wren added Tom Tower to the facade built by Cardinal Wolsey. It is now the most valuable of the pictures, watercolours and photographs that adorn the walls of my room at Hillrise in Worthing – a constant reminder of the four formative years that I enjoyed in the city of dreaming spires, together with a photograph of the cathedral spire that I took from my bedroom window on the top floor of Meadow Buildings.

One sunny afternoon in October 1923, Canon E.W. Watson showed a party of 'freshers' round the college buildings. On the first floor of the Library we were taken into a small room overlooking the Deanery garden. We were told that this was where Lewis Carroll sometimes told his imaginative stories to Alice Liddell and her sisters, although there is no factual evidence for this. Then our guide drew our attention to an orrery in the centre of the room, and asked me to explain what it was and how it worked. How he knew that I was interested in astronomy I shall never know: I had never heard the word 'orrery' before, but it clearly was a model of the solar system, which by turning a handle showed the planets rotating about the Sun, and the Moon rotating about the Earth. It was an ideal instrument for demonstrating how eclipses occur.

Life at Christ Church did not prove to be as expensive as I

feared. One had breakfast in one's own sitting room and could order a hot dish from the kitchen; I provided my own cold lunch, obtaining my victuals from shops or the market in Oxford – my only luxury being a bottle of cider; tea could be had in the Junior Common Room, or brought to one's room when entertaining friends (anchovy toast being a favourite item), or one could go to the Cadena or other tea shops in the city. One had to eat a minimum of four dinners in the Hall each week – they cost 2s 6d each – and the scholars sat at a separate table, whilst the Dean and dons sat at the High Table on a platform, below the painting by Holbein of the reputed 'founder' of the college, King Henry VIII. The Hall, with its portraits of past dignitaries and worthies – including C.L. Dogson's *Lewis Carroll* – is considered to be the finest of all such buildings in Oxford.

I have calculated the total cost of my four years in Oxford. It was my good fortune to receive £80 per annum from the college mathematics scholarship, £40 per annum from the Middlesex County Council, £90 per annum from a school leaving exhibition towards the expenses of three years' residence in college and a year in 'digs' at 229 Abingdon Road. This left about £90 p.a. to be found, as my parents met all my expenses during the vacation, at home in Acton or on holiday at Brixham, Devon, and there was never any suggestion that I should find a vacation job. At that time both of my parents were teaching in LCC schools, and bearing all the expenses of my sister's education at London University, where she obtained a general degree and then spent a year working for a teaching diploma. Subsequently she taught, mainly mathematics, in a number of girls' schools. We both returned home during vacations, but the debt I owe to them is much more than a financial one: they showed us loving kindness throughout our adult lives.

Mr T.W. Chaundy, the mathematical lecturer at Christ Church, was my tutor. We met at the beginning of each term to discuss what books I should read on my own and what courses of lectures I should attend. At the second of my weekly tutorials, I produced some examples from Bell's *Three Dimensional Geometry* that I had worked out, which he returned the next week with the written comment: 'This is very good stuff', but I gathered that he did not wish me to show him some written work each week. So tutorials were spent in discussing difficulties I had met, or introducing a new topic. I was allowed to borrow from my tutor's collection of his mss notes on a variety of topics that had not appeared in print.

There would be one or two lectures to attend each morning at other colleges, mainly at Balliol, Brasenose, Magdalen and New College. At other times I visited all the other men's colleges and churches in the city, because of my interest in architecture. My normal practice was to make notes at each lecture, and later in the day to make a fair copy of them in a note book. One summer term I borrowed a portable typewriter from Emlyn Williams, who also had a room in Meadow Buildings, on Staircase I. He did not mind my using it for several weeks to type my lecture notes, as he was generally busy day and night at the OU Dramatic Society. I then decided to invest in a secondhand Underwood standard typewriter (made in 1905), and had the commercial signs on it replaced by some mathematical symbols – π, Δ, Σ, etc. It has had to be repaired several times during the last 70 years, but it is still usable for writing letters and articles, as well as my recreational mathematics – puzzles needing very elementary knowledge.

I remember especially the lectures by G.E. Hardy at New College on geometry: he used a blackboard and chalk, and after using a duster to clean the board, he would clasp it to his breast, smothering his black gown with white chalk dust, with the result that at the end of a lecture he looked like a living snowman. A course of lectures at Brasenose intrigued me so much that later on I filled a book with about 80 different shapes of cubic curves, dependent upon the number of asymptotes, nodes, etc. Professor Love's lectures on dynamics culminated in his model of a gyroscope made with a bicycle wheel as its chief component.

For my special subject in the final examination I chose cubic surfaces, and attended Professor Dixon's lectures at Magdalen College. On typing out my notes of his proof that there are 27 lines on every cubic surface, I found a short cut at one stage of the prolonged argument. I had the good fortune of being able to introduce this in my answer to the question in the finals examination paper; I expect that it was this bit of original thinking that enabled me to be given a first-class honours degree. I lent these typed notes to my friend H.E. Carpenter, who took the examination a year later, and he told me that they helped him to get a first-class degree too. My tutor told me that I had performed only moderately well on the six papers taken by all candidates in the final examination.

In the evening of the day when I wrote my last examination paper in Oxford, Carpenter and I went by excursion train to Cricceith, hoping to see the total eclipse of the sun. We were disappointed as the sky was overcast early the next morning, but we had put our bicycles in the guard's van, so we were able to make a leisurely return to Oxford, visiting the splendid old castles in North Wales, such as Caernarvon and Conwy, and spending the night at Llanberis at the foot of Snowdon: in the evening we climbed a short distance up the mountain beside the railway track. On the next day we rode up the Llanberis Pass, and ended the day at Harlech village, where we found bed and breakfast in a guest house whose owners conversed in Welsh and had only a nodding acquaintance with the English language. We then took the coastal road south, being ferried across the river at Barmouth, visiting Aberystwyth and the Devil's Dyke. My memory of our exact route has faded after 73 years, but I recollect finding Bed and Breakfast at Builth Wells, crossing the River Severn at

Gloucester and arriving one afternoon at my digs at 229 Abingdon Road to find a pile of letters and telegrams awaiting me: I realised that I had had another stroke of good fortune, and had been awarded a first-class honours degree in mathematics.

Earlier in that year (1928) I had sought a teaching post with the help of the Oxford Appointments Board. I was interviewed at Christ's Hospital, Horsham, and was offered a post if the expected vacancy occurred, and then went on to Sherborne School, Dorset, and was interviewed by Mr Nowell Smith in May; I remember spending the evening playing with his five-year-old daughter on the lounge floor, and being invited to take a class in a geometry lesson the next morning. When I was offered a post for the following September, I gladly accepted, as I had 'fallen in love' with the people and the place, especially as I had learnt that the school had a group of madrigal singers.

My interest in Tudor music was first aroused when in Oxford. The cathedral choir gave recitals of unaccompanied music, either in the Dining Hall, or on the Staircase to the Hall, with the audience seated in Tom Quad on a warm summer's evening. I still possess some of the programmes of the delightful concerts. I also made the acquaintance of the cathedral organist, Dr Henry G. Ley, and was often in the organ gallery during choral Evensong. On weekdays Matins was said at 8 a.m. (attended by a minority of undergraduates), with Choral Evensong, I think, at 5 p.m. On Sundays Holy Communion was said at 8 a.m. followed by Choral Matins and Evensong. My earliest recollection of the music performed is of Haydn's *Insanae et Vanuae Curae*.

I joined the Bach Choir after passing a voice test that revealed my inability to read music easily, and enjoyed the rehearsals at the museum conducted by Sir Hugh Allen. The only remark of his that I can recollect was addressed to the sopranos and altos, who were mostly the wives of dons living in North Oxford – 'SING, you virgins!' The choir gave performances in the Sheldonian Theatre at the end of each term. Thus I enjoyed singing the great choral masterpieces, ranging from Bach's *B Minor Mass* to a first performance of Vaughan William's *Sancta Civitas*. Another source of musical pleasure was provided by the Sunday evening piano recitals in the hall of Balliol College, where I first heard Beethoven's piano sonatas.

For a short time I joined the St Aldate's Choral Society, where we sang part-songs and a choral version of Bizet's *Carmen*. Another recollection is of hearing an early gramophone record of Beethoven's *Fifth Symphony*, played at coffee time in Ellison's Restaurant.

I must confess that I wasted some of my time in college. My foolish youthful pranks included climbing on to the roof of the buildings in Tom Quad near the cathedral, from where I gained access to the clerestory of the cathedral through a small unlocked wooden door. One winter's day I was in the clerestory during a choir practice, and a boy spotted a movement and that started a rumour about a cathedral ghost.

Some days later Dr Ley gave a special recital from 8 to 9 p.m. for the benefit of 'members of the House' (mainly undergraduates). When it was over we all left by the 'tunnel' into Tom Quad, and Dr Ley switched off the gaslights that illuminated the interior of the cathedral. I went back to my rooms with some friends, and took them into my bedroom to see the dreaming spires of Oxford by night. To our surprise we saw that bright light was coming from the clerestory windows of the cathedral quire – clearly visible less than 100 yards away. We went to report the matter to the porter at Tom Gate, who came with his bunch of keys to the 'tunnel', and he could see that the whole of the interior of the cathedral was illuminated, but when one of us mentioned that perhaps the cathedral ghost was responsible, he refused to unlock the door, exclaiming, 'Ghost! There's no such thing as ghosts.' The gaslights were still burning the next morning when the verger arrived to open up.

Another prank was to ascend the stairway up to the belfry of Tom Tower and stand on top of the huge bell when the hammer struck the bell to indicate the hour. Every evening all colleges shut their gates when Tom finished tolling 101 times: I do not know whether this was done by a human ringer or by some automatic mechanism, and no ghost was blamed when it was rumoured that on one occasion more than 101 strokes were heard. When concerts were performed it was essential that an interval in the programme occurred about 9 o'clock.

My knowledge of vocal music had been greatly increased as Dr E.H. Fellowes was at that time engaged upon publishing Tudor music, both sacred and secular, and for the first time in centuries Weelkes' impressive *Hosanna to the Son of David* and *Gloria in excelsis Deo* could be heard in 'choirs and places where they sing' throughout the world.

Revival of interest in Tudor music had begun in Victorian times, when Novello printed a number of madrigals, edited by Victorian musicians who often thought their version improved upon the original. Authenticity was restored; many years later Walter S. Collins gained his doctorate of music at an American university, as a result of a year's research into the church music of Thomas Weelkes, and he discovered the original six parts of an anthem that Dr Fellowes had published after reconstructing the missing second treble part. His reconstruction was about 90 per cent correct.

When my last day in Oxford arrived, I sent my luggage home by train, and rode the 50 miles back to London on my bicycle – a present from my parents on my twenty-first birthday.

4

Sherborne School

I was appointed as the fifth mathematical member of the staff at Sherborne School in the spring of 1927, several weeks before I took my final mathematical examination at Oxford. The only evidence of my suitability for the post must have been my school testimonial, which I recall spoke of my achievement as CSM of the school OTC during my final year. Probably my tutor at Christ Church, Oxford – Mr T.W. Chaundy – was consulted. But as I had not spent a year at a training college for teachers and obtained a certificate, I relied upon the books published by the Mathematical Association on the teaching of arithmetic, algebra, geometry, calculus, etc, books by Percy Nunn and Godfrey and Siddon, and an American book on teaching generally.

I have no recollection now of how I travelled from London to begin my three years' residence at Tantallon, Acreman Street, Sherborne, where Mrs Pope had three sets of room for masters. A few years previously I had cycled with my father and sister from Acton to Brixham, Devon, spending one night in Salisbury. I still have a clear picture in my mind's eye of the first glimpse of the cathedral spire from a distance, as we rounded a hill some miles away. By the time we reached Salisbury the cathedral was closed, and I stayed on the next morning to visit it, whilst my father and sister went ahead to Sherborne, where I caught them up about midday to have a picnic lunch together. As there was still about 70 miles to travel to Brixham, I think I had no time even to enter the Abbey Church, and so my first visit to Sherborne was indeed a flying one. I have no idea what route we took for our return journey home a month later.

In all probability in September 1927 I sent my luggage by train, and cycled from Acton to Sherborne.

R.S. Thompson and J.H. Randolph occupied the other sets of room during my first term at Tantallon. In the second year they were replaced by A.B. Gourlay and H.C.W. Davis, but when the former left to become assistant at School House, and the latter married a nurse who tended him whilst he was in the Yeatman hospital, I was left alone for my final year.

I was immediately put in charge of a small group of boys studying mathematics and science up to university scholarship level. My method of teaching them was based on what I had experienced myself at St Paul's School and at Oxford. As I have mentioned, Mr Chaundy had compiled mss sets of notes on a variety of mathematical topics, which he lent to his students, so I compiled similar mss sets of notes, introductory to new topics, such as determinants. I also taught sets of young boys, and the second set of School Certificate boys, who were expected to pass that examination without difficulty, whilst the bright boys in the first set also took some of the 'additional papers' in more advanced topics, and the third and fourth sets were in the care of two older and experienced teachers. The head of the mathematical department was 'Ben' Davis, who looked after the army class. He was one of the trio of Davises – Ben, Hen and Len – the two latter being a scientist (biologist) and the head of the art department respectively.

All did well during my first year in their respective examinations.

Meanwhile my sister Doreen, having obtained a general degree at London University, continued for a year and obtained a Teacher's Certificate. She then gave me all the books she had studied during the course, and I was able to 'train myself' by reading them with great interest. A book on psychology by MacDougall fascinated me so much that I bought his book on abnormal psychology and books on mental tests.

During my first few years I visited a different classroom for each set, but eventually I was granted the sole use of a room in a house just outside the main entrance, where I had a bookcase for my mathematical library.

I had been advised by friends not to regard my first teaching post as a permanent appointment, but to treat it as a time in which to acquire the art of teaching. One of my contemporaries at school and Christ Church taught classics at Sherborne for one term, and then returned to join the staff at St Paul's School for the rest of his days till retirement.

In 1928 I made applications for two posts. The first was Head of Mathematics at the Royal Naval College at Dartmouth, for which I was interviewed by the Head, who was due to retire. I was delighted to learn that he had a gramophone and records in his classroom, and I got the impression that I was the kind of successor they were looking for; but when I told him that I hoped to be ordained and become a school chaplain, he said that the Navy always appointed a full-time chaplain, and I felt compelled to withdraw my application – I could not expect to be granted leave of absence for a year to attend a theological college.

There was a vacancy for a lecturer at Newcastle University. When I was interviewed there, I was a little alarmed when told that I would be expected to do some research besides lecturing, as I doubted my ability to do more than pass on the knowledge I had already acquired; there would also be the problem of obtaining a year's leave of absence to study for ordination, so I withdrew my application.

* * *

During the Easter holiday in 1928 I went with two Oxford friends on a week's cycle tour in Normandy; as I no longer have the maps and guide book which we used, I have to rely wholly on the rather dim memories of over 70 years ago. We were three mathematicians, two from Brasenose College, one being my life-long school friend Carp, and the other a friend of his, Cowling.

We crossed the Channel to St Malo, arriving in time to make the short journey to Mont St Michel, near which we stayed the first night. Next morning we returned to Mont St Michel and had a guided tour of the monastery and visited a shop where I had an opportunity to use my knowledge of the French language when buying a small souvenir. We used to buy food for our meals during the day, including a bottle of cheap wine, and enjoyed a full evening meal at the hotels where we spent the nights.

Our aim was to visit as many of the cities in Normandy where there were cathedrals – Lisieux, Caen, Rouen, etc. and I have pleasant memories of our stay at Coutances, near Rouen, a picturesque village with fine old houses.

At Caen we saw the two abbeys, climbing the tower of one of them and seeing the famous Bayeux tapestry. The weather was settled, and I have no recollection of being held up by rain.

We sailed from Le Havre by a night boat, landed in England and set off to our various homes separately. I remember a strong head-wind which so exhausted me that when I reached Alton I made my way to the station, intending to complete my journey by train, but a Sherborne boy spotted me as I rode down the high street and caught me up before I reached the station. After a cup of coffee and a chat I was able to complete the remainder of my journey to London.

I was glad to remain at Sherborne, and read the books for the first part of the General Ordination Examination on my own, and answered the papers in the Headmaster's study. Later I was granted six months' leave of absence to attend two terms at Ripon Hall.

Seven years later I learnt that a little theological knowledge is a dangerous thing, and that *odium theologicum* makes some men into religious bigots, devoid of the elementary Christian virtue of charity.

I was disappointed to learn that Mr Nowell Smith had notified the school governors of his intention to retire at the end of my first term and return to Oxford, where I believe he was a Fellow of New College. The number of boys at the school had increased greatly during his headmastership, and it ranked amongst the country's well-known public boarding schools. My colleagues told me that he had endeavoured to raise the academic standard of the school, whilst a group of assistant masters thought that the school's reputation depended upon its achievements in sport, especially rugby football. In their opinion Mr Nowell Smith would have remained had he known that the leader of the 'rugger group', a housemaster named Carey, would die a few weeks after the autumn term had begun – he was reputed to have been a university rugger blue. Some of the assistant masters had been appointed because of their achievements in various sports, and therefore their ability to organise the school games, whilst 'academics' such as myself would only act as umpires at cricket or referees at rugger.

Every morning the boys assembled in the courtyard to do physical exercises under the guidance of Max Westlake, who was in charge of Elmdene, a boarding house for some new boys awaiting places in one of the main boarding houses; he was the only housemaster who ever invited me to visit a dormitory full of boys in bed, just before 'lights out'.

I was soon on friendly terms with all the other masters, especially with Mr W.A.T. Jarrett, who lived next door to Tantallon with his wife, who regularly invited me to supper on Sunday evenings, and I assisted with the washing up as a drier. The three of us also went to play bridge with Mrs Hamilton, a housemistress at the girls' school. On one occasion our hostess arranged a bridge tournament, in which she assigned me to partner the Headmistress. We had the good fortune to win the tournament.

On many afternoons I played fives with A.B. Gourlay. We visited Clifton School once to play a doubles match against two of the staff, and just managed to win – thanks to the superhuman energy of my partner. On Saturday afternoons I enjoyed playing cricket in the Sherborne Town 2nd XI but did not achieve distinction with bat or ball. My best achievement was to make three catches on a village ground with a slope that hid the stumps from view.

My other activity outside the school was with the Sherborne Amateur Operatic and Dramatic Society, which was supported by a number of vice-presidents, including the Headmaster, the Chaplain and others connected with the school. I was one of the 'Gentlemen of Japan' in the 1930 production of *The Mikado* at the Carlton Theatre in Sherborne, and sang in the chorus of *Patience* in 1932. The society then lapsed until 1937, when it revived with a production of *The Gondoliers*. I shared the title roles with Gerald Ellison, the curate at the Abbey, as Giuseppi (baritone) and myself as Marco (tenor). R.S. Thompson was the Grand Inquisitor, and Casilda was acted by Margaret King, wife of a Sherborne master. We gave seven performances to full houses, and 'Take a Pair of Sparkling Eyes' received its traditional encore.

At a school performance of *Trial by Jury* I was one of the jurymen. The only things I still remember were the cry of 'Silence in Court' by the Usher, J.H. Randolph, and R.S. Thompson as the Judge.

In December 1928 I was invited to participate in a production of *Dances, Mimes and Songs* by Mary King, the daughter of the Revd J.H. King, a retired Sherborne schoolmaster. I took the tenor part in a vocal quartet that sang three unaccompanied part songs, and five nursery rhymes set to music by Walford Davies – just two of fifteen items. I enjoyed my first experience of ballet music led by Mary King, who was a professional dance teacher and fairy-like solo performer. I can recollect the joy of this, my first appearance in public as a singer.

I sang with the school chapel choir, and with the choral society. At the end of each autumn term there was a festival of nine lessons and carols held in the Abbey Church. In the 1934 programme I see the words of old English, French and German carols, including the full Latin text of *Quem Pastores Laudavere*, and more modern English hymns. School concerts by visiting artistes were frequently arranged by the Director of Music, Mr B.J. Francis Picton, one of which was given by Jelly D'Aranyl, the violinist, a personal friend of Mr Nowell Smith. In an undated programme I see my name amongst a group of ten unaccompanied singers, who sang a Soprano/Alto/Tenor/Bass version of John Dowland's lute song, *Wilt thou unkind thus reave me?* – probably this was the group that occasionally met to sing madrigals under Mr Picton. In 1935 the Madrigal Club sang Tomkins' madrigal *Weep no more, thou sorry boy*.

Although I had an abundance of musical activities at the school, I also joined the Templecombe Choral Society, conducted by Gwen Windsor, the daughter of Prebendary Windsor, the rector. For several years I travelled each week by car for the rehearsal, preceded by dinner at the Rectory. The choir took part in the South Somerset Competitive Festival – with what success I cannot now recollect. But I have the programme of a concert given in the village hall, which included a short sketch, 'The Jumble Sale', presumably for the benefit of villagers who would find a recital of vocal and instrumental music a little tedious. I see that two old English melodies arranged by Lane-Wilson were sung by the Revd D.B. Eperson, and piano, violin and cello soloists contributed to a wide variety of pieces, ranging from Orlandus Lassus to Vaughan Williams. I thoroughly enjoyed these excursions, despite the fact that on one occasion my car grazed another on a bend in a country lane, and on another night I ran into flood water on the main road that sent a wave over the windscreen and brought the car to a temporary halt.

In the commemoration programme for 1938 (my final year in Sherborne), honours obtained by past and present Shirburnians are recorded: Alan Turing, a mathematical scholar and later fellow of King's College, Cambridge, had been elected to a travelling fellowship to Princeton University, USA; D.G. Christopherson, a mathematical-scientist, had obtained a first-class degree in engineering and a Henry Fellowship at Oxford: P.H. Geake, a mathematical exhibitioner at Trinity Hall, Cambridge, had obtained first-class honours in the mathematical tripos, part I. Four new scholarships obtained during 1937–8 included an organ scholarship at Pembroke College, Cambridge, won by H.T. Fry.

These honours seem to indicate that the academic standards at the school had risen during the past ten years, as Mr Nowell Smith had hoped; 21 candidates had obtained Higher School Certificates, with 6 distinctions, and 128 candidates for the School Certificate had obtained 121 certificates, with an average of 4 credits each.

During my 11 years I had been responsible for a class of boys studying for the School Certificate; there were about 100 boys of this age, divided, as I have said, into four groups. I had just one unexpected failure with my second set – a bright boy who, according to my mark book, was amongst the top eight boys in the weekly orders, and who passed easily when he took the examination again in the next term.

I was also responsible for a lower school group of about 16 new boys – 13 to 14 years of age. After the end-of-term examination in December I compiled a mathematical crossword puzzle, the clues being simple problems in arithmetic such as we had met during the term's work. To my amazement the first boy to produce a complete solution was the one who had consistently been bottom of the class throughout the term, and I thought he was one of those unfortunate human beings who have 'a mathematical blind spot'. His name was the same as that of a well-known Tudor lyrical poet, from whom he believed he was descended. In class he had a dreamy look, as of one that was contemplating higher matters than arithmetic calculations.

From this incident I learnt the lesson that recreational mathematics were of value in the classroom. The first article that I wrote for *The Times Educational Supplement*, given the title 'Puzzling it out' by the Editor, was based upon this experience. In my lessons I would frequently digress into talking about astronomy and space travel possibilities (this was many years before it became a reality), or how sound was recorded on a gramophone record. I soon began inviting small groups of boys to come to my sitting room to hear records of classical music played on an electrically operated HMV gramophone, which was a great advance upon the original hand-wound machine with a large horn, as pictured on HMV products.

I was put in charge of the small class of boys specialising in mathematics, which included a brilliant teenager, Christopher Morcom, who won a scholarship at Trinity College, Cambridge, in December 1930, but tragically died after a minor operation the following February.

5

Educating a Mathematical Genius

Alan Turing at Sherborne School

(From *Mathematics in School*, May 1994)

by Canon D.B. Eperson

(Member of Staff at Sherborne School, 1927–1939)

Two conflicting biographies and a BBC TV programme about Dr Alan Turing – the pioneer designer of the electronic computer, *ACE* – describing his activities from his schooldays until his mysterious early death, have prompted me to record my recollections of the budding mathematical genius during this time at Sherborne School.

Mrs Sara Turing wrote a biography of her son shortly after his death at the age of 42 years, which she regarded as "accidental". In 1983 Andrew Hodges published a much more detailed book, entitled: "*Alan Turing: the Enigma*", motivated by his interest in mathematics and in the Gay Liberation Movement. His verdict was that Turing's death was suicidal: "*The story of Alan Turing's life ... does show intelligence thwarted and destroyed by its environment.*"

This opinion may or may not be valid as regards his adult life, but it is certainly not true that when a boy at Sherborne School his intellectual development was hampered by his public school environment. The author of the biography did not conceal his prejudice against public school education, and his criticism of a distinguished headmaster and his staff at the time when Turing was at Sherborne School were extremely biased. It would be unfortunate if present-day mathematicians accepted his view that Turing was adversely affected by his experience at a boarding school, whereas his mother was completely satisfied by the intellectual and moral training he received.

The author's criticism of my colleagues was also unfair: some of them had made critical remarks on Turing's attitude towards subjects other than Science and Mathematics, but photocopies of his school reports and School Certificate Examination results show that his all-round ability was recognised.

In the biography there are several references to me as Turing's mathematical tutor: although they do not err on the side of flattery, they are devoid of the venom of his remarks about other masters.

In September 1927, I joined the school staff and taught sets of boys of all ages, including a group of six who were beginning their study of the syllabus of Higher School Certificate mathematics. The most promising was Christopher Morcom, who obtained 85 per cent of the marks in the examination I set at the end of a year.

I first met Alan Turing in the Summer term of 1928, at the end of which he took the School Certificate Examination. My end of term report stated that *"He has been reading for the Additional Mathematics papers more or less on his own, and should do well"*.

Having passed the School Certificate Examination with flying colours, Turing joined the select group of budding mathematicians, and in December I reported that *"This term has been spent, and the next two terms will have to be spent, in filling in the many gaps in his knowledge, and* organising *it. He thinks very rapidly and is apt to be 'brilliant' but unsound in some of his work. He is seldom defeated by a problem, but his methods are often crude, cumbersome and untidy, but thoroughness and polish will no doubt come in time"*. The Headmaster added the comment: *"This report is full of promise"*.

In January 1929 an older boy, Pat Mermagen, joined the group after he had won a Cambridge Scholarship. They all took the Higher School Certificate Examination in the following July, when the marks obtained were:- Morcom 1436, Mermagen 1365, Turing 1033 and some "also rans".

All three continued in September, as Mermagen had elected to stay on as Captain of the School and Captain of Rugby and Cricket. Morcom took the Cambridge Scholarship Examination in December and was awarded one at Trinity College, but he died tragically in the following February after an operation. In July Mermagen obtained 1140 marks, and Turing 1079 in the HBC Examination.

Turing shared my admiration for the undoubted talent of Morcom, his senior by one year, and hoped to emulate him by gaining a mathematical scholarship at Trinity College, Cambridge. Their friendship had been a source of mutual benefit, and Morcom's influence on the young genius was all to his good.

1930–31 was Turing's final year at school, during which he gained a scholarship at King's College, Cambridge. I was glad that the examiners were able to perceive his talent, since on paper his solutions were often unorthodox. In July his HSC marks reached only 1079; these figures show that Turing, though potentially a gifted mathematician, never did really well in the conventional HSC topics.

In one sense he was difficult to teach, as he preferred to make his own independent investigations. He was reputed to have "discovered" Gregory's series $\frac{\pi}{4} = 1 - \frac{1}{3} + \frac{1}{5} - \frac{1}{7} +$ ad inf., without using calculus during his early school days. He was less interested in studying textbooks and developing a good style.

On the other hand he was an industrious member of the class, who needed no stimulus to exert himself mentally, and he could readily appreciate the solution that I showed him to any problem that he could not solve by the light of nature, i.e. by discovering his own alternative method.

I believe that my deliberate policy of leaving him mainly to his own devices, and standing by to assist when necessary, allowed his mathematical genius to progress uninhibited. I cannot recollect that he ever made use of my classroom library of books on a variety of mathematical and scientific topics, but obviously he read and understood books on advanced topics, such as Relativity.

Out of school I had little contact with Turing, as I do not think that he showed any interest in school games or in music-making, or in the activities of the school Archaeological Society and the Gramophone Society that I organised. His friendly rival Morcom came regularly to the record recitals in my rooms on Sunday afternoons, whilst other boys helped me to run the Cinema Society, and to operate the formidable apparatus that HMV produced at my request to fill the school hall with sounds from records.

When at Sherborne I soon realised the value of "*Recreational Mathematics*" in the classroom, and so "side-tracks" such as Astronomy and Space Travel were occasionally explored. I still have the notebook that I compiled during 1927–39 containing topics such as Dissections, Magic Squares, Knight's Tours on a Chessboard, exotic Envelopes, Recurring Decimal

Patterns, Factorising Symmetrical Determinants and Indeterminate Equations of the 1st and 2nd degrees. By word and by example I encouraged boys to investigate problems and puzzles on their own, and to enjoy their mathematical activities.

I certainly enjoyed my own varied activities as a young master, both inside and outside the classroom, and have pleasant recollections of the friendly attitude of boys and colleagues. I can endorse the opinion of another master, A.J.P. Andrews, quoted in Mrs Turing's book, that Christopher Morcom and Alan Turing were the most brilliant boys that it was our privilege to teach at school.

Sherborne School should be given credit for providing an environment in which a budding scientifically minded mathematician was happy, and could develop his talents and grow in knowledge and maturity.

References
Hodges, A (1983) *Alan Turing – The Enigma*, Burnett Books.

POSTSCRIPT

I am grateful to the editor of the Sherborne School magazine, *The Shirburnian*, for printing this article, which I wrote after listening to a BBC programme on the life of Alan Turing, and reading the biography entitled *Alan Turing – The Enigma*, both of which in my opinion gave a distorted view of the life at school of the young mathematical genius.

In conclusion to this review of the life of Alan Turing at Sherborne School here are some quotations from some of his school reports that have survived.

'*Summer, 1929*. Mathematics. His work on Higher Certificate

Papers shows distinct promise, but he must realise that ability to put a neat and tidy solution on paper is necessary for a first-rate mathematician.'

'*Summer, 1930.* Mathematics. He has faced the uninspiring task of revision and consolidation of his previous knowledge with determination, and I think he has improved his style of written work, which is more convincing and less sketchy than last year. If he does not get flustered and relapse into slip-shod work, he should do very well in H.C. this year.'

I was absent at Ripon Hall, Oxford, preparing for ordination, during the Michaelmas term 1930, but my deputy made an almost illegible report:

'Mathematics. A really able mathematician. His trouble is his untidiness and poor style, but he has tried hard to improve in this. He sometimes fails over a simple problem by trying to do it by complicated methods instead of by an elementary one.' At the end of this term he took the Scholarship Examination, Cambridge, and was awarded a Scholarship at King's College.

'*Lent term, 1931.* He has done some post-scholarship reading without encountering any serious difficulties. He should be able to take the Higher Certificate next July in his stride.'

'*Summer, 1931.* He has gone on with his reading as well as revising the elementary work for the Higher Certificate, and I expect him to get a Distinction with ease. He has my best wishes for an equally successful career at Cambridge.'

6

Leisure-Time Activities

Shortly after my arrival I was asked to take over the organisation of the long-established school Archaeological Society: this involved arranging six lectures by visiting experts during the autumn and spring terms, and three expeditions to places of interest in Dorset, Somerset and Wiltshire. The first expedition for which I was solely responsible was on May 17th, 1928, for which I prepared a foolscap sheet of information of the places to be visited, together with a sketch map of the route – Yeovil, Beaminster, Bridport, West Bay, Eype Down and Golden Cap, Abbotsbury (church, barn, gardens, swannery), Chesil Beach, Weymouth. The boys shared the cost of hiring the coaches. This expedition was repeated four years later with the next generation of boys. The return journey from Weymouth passed through Dorchester and up the Cerne valley, through Charminster and past the Cerne Giant.

Another expedition worth mention was to Stonehenge, Old Sarum and Salisbury Cathedral, and I shall never forget visiting Wookey Hole, the Cheddar Caves, Wells Cathedral and Glastonbury Abbey.

A colleague lent me an album of records of Puccini's opera *La Bohème*. I duplicated copies of a summary of the libretto, and played some of the records to a room full of boys at Tantallon one Sunday afternoon. These recitals were so much appreciated that I decided to organise a Gramophone Society with a record player capable of filling the school hall with sound. The Headmaster made me a grant of £100 (presumably from school funds and not out of his own pocket). I contacted HMV and asked for a design of a machine that would fulfil my purposes – at a cost of £100. When it arrived it consisted of three separate heavy boxes connected by yards of cables. Membership of the Gramophone Society cost 2s 6d per term. The money was used to build up a library of records, kept in my classroom, from which a member could borrow a few records each week to play in his own room. The music at the Sunday afternoon recitals was chosen and presented by members of the staff – both amateur and professional musicians.

About this time cinema 'talkies' were invented, and early in the 1930s small projectors for home use were on the market. With the aid of a £100 grant I bought a 'home talkie' machine, and formed a Cinema Society. The 2s 6d per term membership fees were used for the hire of educational and feature films for showing in the school hall on Saturday evening. The boys operated the projector and moved the silver screen – all I had to do was to choose the films from a catalogue, and post them back to London on the following Monday. These ventures proved to be successful, and during my last year I was asked to form a Chess Club – a request I had to refuse, as all my spare time was taken with preparing for going to Charminster and furnishing a large Victorian vicarage.

Shortly before I left Sherborne the Headmaster summoned me to his study, and I wondered whether he wished to thank me for all the extra work I had done in contributing to the cultural activities of the school. I expected no thanks, and received none.

It is time now to turn the clock back more than ten years and report on the appointment of Mr D.L.F. Boughy as successor to Nowell Smith as headmaster. He was a bachelor – an ex-Guardsman who had been a successful housemaster at Marlborough College. Shortly after his arrival in January 1928 I told him of my wish to be ordained, and he was most sympathetic and helpful, I read all the text books for Part I of the General Ordination Examination, and he allowed me to write my answers to the papers on the Old and New Testaments, Church history, ethics, the Book of Common Prayer, etc. in his study. He then allowed me leave of absence for one autumn term, so that I could go to Ripon Hall, Oxford, to study for the second part of the GOE.

There were about 16 students, most of them younger than myself, but one older man in his forties, John Clifton Barker, who found 'going back to school' rather a strain, He knew no Greek, and so he was excused studying the New Testament in its original language, and even to study the Vulgate, the Latin translation, presented him with problems, so I used to help him with his task. My simple plan was for him to memorise as much as he could of the Authorised Version of the Gospels and Epistles, and to be able to recognise Latin words, such as *crucifixus*, which have similar words in English. We would read together a passage from the Vulgate, and he would try to spot the key Latin words we had previously found, and that would remind him of a passage in the Authorised Version, and enable him to 'translate' the whole passage into English. I left Oxford and he continued at Ripon Hall. He was ordained about two years later, and served curacies in the diocese of Rochester, ending his years of ministry as rector of a parish near King's Lynn. I used to visit him during vacations whilst my home was in Acton.

I was ordained deacon in Salisbury Cathedral in December 1930 with the title Assistant Chaplain at Sherborne School, and priest the following year. Mr Boughey's next kindness was to pay me the difference between my normal salary for a term and what he had paid to the master who deputised for me!

My clerical duties were very small: I conducted chapel

services occasionally on weekdays and Sundays, alternating with the Chaplain, a retired parish priest, and a former ordained housemaster – both of them old Shirburnians. I preached once each term – my inspiration being a book of sermons by Nowell Smith, entitled *Members One of Another.* Preparation of boys for confirmation was undertaken by housemasters, unless parents asked for their son to be prepared by a priest. But I soon found that assistance with services on Sundays at nearby village churches were appreciated by the Vicar of Sherborne Abbey, who was also responsible for two small churches in Sherborne and at Lillington, to which I was conveyed by car together with a young lady organist.

On my first visit to the tiny church at Lillington, I could not see a lectern, and was searching in vain for a Bible in the priest's stall during the singing of the psalms, when the verger came to my rescue. I told him of my problem: 'Bible?' he enquired. 'Vicar do keep 'e in the pulpit,' was his enlightening reply.

The frequency of the requests for assistance on Sundays led me to think that it would save the trouble of transport being needed if I had my own car, I felt that this extravagance would be justifiable, and accordingly a friend took me for a drive in a Citroën 7 – the 'clover leaf' model with seating for a driver and two passengers. He showed me how to operate the pedals and brakes – using double declutching when changing gear. So I bought one for £8 and spent a few days practising on the roads around Sherborne. A week later I drove to Oxford to attend a Gaudy, and parked my small vehicle in Christ Church Meadows, alongside the opulent cars owned by other old members of the House.

I painted the bodywork green and the wings a darker shade of green, but alas! After a few months exploring Dorset, its main axle broke, and I had to replace it with a secondhand Ford that cost at least twice as much. This was a four-seater, and I was able to take passengers with me on visits to the coast – Weymouth, Portland, Durdle Door (now seen daily on BBC

TV during morning news bulletins), Lulworth Cove, the Isle of Purbeck, etc. On one occasion I ran out of petrol on the high road to Dorchester on a Sunday afternoon, and had to walk a mile or so down to the Cerne valley and obtain a can of petrol from the garage at the north end of Charminster. I had three boys with me, and we managed to return to Sherborne in time for Evensong.

My visits to neighbouring village churches were not without incidents still clear in my memory. I record here just two of them. I was asked to conduct a wedding one Saturday afternoon at Milborne Port, just across the border in Somerset. When we went into the vestry at the end of the service in order to sign the marriage registers, we found that they were in the locked safe and the vicar had gone off with the keys. The newly married couple had to depart on their honeymoon without a marriage certificate.

In the vestry of Trent Church after an evening service, a churchwarden expressed regret that I had said that the Bible was untrue; the theme of my sermon was 'moral courage', and as an instance of this Christian virtue I cited the Victorian Bishop Colenso, who was the first prelate of the Church of England who stated publicly that the first chapter of Genesis was mythical and not historical. On many other occasions I was thanked for my 'interesting address', which I remember on one occasion was about the Revd C.L. Dodgson, alias Lewis Carroll.

Once I conducted the morning service at Castleton Church, and preached to a congregation from Sherborne girls' school. On another Sunday morning I went to the corrugated iron church on the fringe of Sherborne, locally known as 'the Tin Tabernacle', and several years later I was invited to dedicate the new organ there.

My first car was nicknamed 'Alphonse' for obvious reasons, and the second car was called 'Old Bill'. In January 1934 I took my sister back to Sutton-on-Sea, where she had a post at a girls' school, in Old Bill. I spent the night at a hotel in a town near Lincoln, and in the next morning visited Lincoln Cathedral for the first time, and took a photograph of the fine west front from the top of the ruined castle. My return route to London was through Stamford, Oundle, Bedford and Luton, in days when motoring was a pleasure, there being only a few cars and small vans on the main roads. In the previous summer when my parents had spent their usual summer holiday at Brixham, I took the whole family to stay for a week at a boarding house in Newquay, which we used as a centre for touring throughout the Cornish peninsula from Land's End to the Lizard. My father and I knew from our cycle tour (see p. 45) where best to go to introduce my mother and sister to that beautiful county.

In the same year I stayed in Gravesend, where my friend the Revd J.C. Barker was a curate at the parish church, but an intended tour to Folkestone, via Rochester, Maidstone and Canterbury, terminated at Elham, where I spent most of the day whilst the car was being repaired. Elham is a picturesque village with a fine church, in which many years later I conducted services during an interregnum.

When Old Bill died of old age, he was succeeded by 'Clarence', a Morris Cowley saloon. In my *Pocket Road Atlas* dated December 1934 I have recorded numerous short tours from Sherborne through towns in Dorset, Wiltshire and Somerset, and a longer tour through Taunton to Minehead, Lynmouth, Combe Martin and across Exmoor. The only other tour recorded was a visit to Gravesend. I have no record of how and when Clarence perished, and was succeeded by a Morris Minor that lasted several years.

Undoubtedly the leisure-time activity that I enjoyed most in Sherborne was singing madrigals and motets with a small group of experienced singers during my last few years. I have no record of the date when the SSAATB group first met: the four ladies were members of the staff of the girls' school (two of them professional music teachers), the bass was R.S. Thompson (a member of the boys' school staff) and myself as tenor. Later we were joined by Gerald Ellison (baritone) when he arrived to be curate at Sherborne Abbey. Edith Little and Joan Ovenden were the sopranos, Mary Willmott and Peggy Dunkley the contraltos. We met each Wednesday in my sitting room at Tantallon from 8 to 10 p.m. I acted as leader and merely started each item indicating the tempo, and the length of the final chord. We were all good sight readers of music, and could unanimously follow the changes of rhythm, pace and volume of sound indicated by the editor in the vocal score. Each meeting provided the highlight of the week for me: participating in the making of music from the Tudor period – the Golden Age of English music.

In 1937 the four ladies, myself and Mr Martin as a deputy bass, since by that time Gerald Ellison had left Sherborne to be Chaplain to the Bishop of Winchester, and R.C. Thompson was playing cricket with the Dorset County XI, attended the Summer School of Music at Downe House, a girls' boarding school near Newbury. The coach for the madrigal and motet course was Dr Middleton of Cambridge, who conducted rehearsals with all the singers during the first part of the morning, and left the second part for individual groups to practise together, In the afternoons we were free to play tennis, go swimming or rambling in the countryside or just snooze, whatever we wished. In the early evening students taking any of the courses (e.g. solo singing or instrumental playing) would assemble in the hall for a rehearsal of a major choral work. Later in the evening a large number of singers would meet to sing madrigals and motets to their heart's content, under Mr Gordon Duff, the expert leader of a madrigal group.

*   *   *

Exhilarating performances by the massed singers of Weelkes' magnificent anthems *Hosanna to the Son of David*, and *Gloria in excelsis Deo* were a joy to me, as such compositions for six voices to be sung by cathedral choirs were not in our repertory. At the final concert the small Sherborne madrigal group contributed *When David heard that Absalom was slain*, set to music by Thomas Tomkins; it was performed without a conductor, received applause from the audience, and praise from the coach and Mr Duff afterwards. This began our friendship with Mr Duff, which flourished in later years when we moved to Canterbury in 1964.

This was the last occasion that our group sang together, as three of the ladies left Sherborne for other posts, and only Peggy Dunkley, R.S. Thompson and I remained, Fortunately Peggy Dunkley found a new member of the staff at the girls' school, Miss Phyllis May Perrett, a Cambridge mathematician, to join the remnants of the group, when they met at Greenhill House. She was a skilled soprano with a pure voice, and an excellent sight reader. She greatly impressed me at this first meeting, and after our second meeting at Tantallon I began to wonder whether she was possibly a suitable partner for life, and before I left Sherborne to become the bachelor Vicar of Charminster we had become engaged to be married – the greatest stroke of good fortune that I was ever given.

Once again I must put the clock back ten years and record my gratitude to Mr Boughey for his kindness to me, which I am sure he extended to other people, such as the boys under his care at School House. He was a gentle man, and it is said that he took to drink because of the strain of conflict with members of the Old Shirburnian Society. He retired, and shortly afterwards he died of cirrhosis of the liver.

His successor, Alexander Ross Wallace, was a very different kind of man. If I may use a canine metaphor, he was like a bulldog, in contrast with the spaniel who preceded him. We were told (unofficially) that his previous experience had been as a Civil Servant in India, and that when India was freed from British domination, he bought a preparatory school in Scotland with the lump sum compensation from the British Government.

This venture was so successful that before long he was appointed Headmaster at Blundell's School. He had hardly settled in, when the Governors of Sherborne School offered him the vacant post at Sherborne, which he accepted. It was rumoured that the salary at Sherborne was much the same as the headmasters at the most famous boarding schools received.

I well remember the first staff meeting over which he presided in the Lower Library, when he apologised for having to announce that the Governors had decided that all members of the academic staff, himself included, were to have a cut in their salaries – because of circumstances over which they had no control.

The only teaching that he undertook was the Sunday morning divinity period: he chose the sixth form of scientists and mathematicians, and I became responsible for the sixth form classicists in studying the Greek New Testament. Mr Wallace was an amateur theologian, with knowledge ranging from the writings of St Thomas Aquinas to William Paley, author of a famous Victorian book of proofs of the existence of God. I believe he had himself published a book entitled *The Seven Pillars of Wisdom*.

At first I had no fixed classroom in which to take the various groups of boys to whom I taught mathematics throughout the school, but by this time I had been allotted a room in an old house just outside the main entrance to the school courtyard. I was passing through this entrance one afternoon when a breathless boy rushed up to me, and blurted out: 'Please, sir, whatever shall I do?' When he had recovered his breath, he continued, 'I've lost my belief in God!' After a long pause he continued, '...notes.'

I solemnly replied, 'Then the sooner you find them the better.' Exit grinning boy.

One Sunday morning the Headmaster's sermon in chapel was on the iniquity of divorce. During the following week a senior boy came to ask me whether I thought that the reason why he, a house prefect, had not been made a school prefect, was because his parents had been divorced. I could not tell him the reason why he had not been promoted, but I met his mother in London and discussed the matter with her.

At some time in 1937, a frightened boy came to tell me that in a lesson period the Headmaster had said that a second war with Germany was inevitable, and the present generation of schoolboys would suffer the same fate as the young men in World War I. I could not allay his fears, but I made contact with his mother, who was living alone in London.

In this case the Headmaster's prediction of the inevitability of war was correct, and although the number of casualties amongst fighting men was less than in World War I, far more civilians lost their lives through the bombing of London and many other cities and towns in England, Nevertheless about 100 new names were added to the School War Memorial – several of boys whom I had taught.

In that same year, 1937, R.S. Thompson told me about an incident in the Masters' Common Room during the mid-morning break. A colleague asked the Headmaster whether he had heard about the fire at Ripon Hall, which caused little damage and endangered no lives. Mr Wallace replied that he had heard, then added, 'It's a pity that the Principal and all his heretics were not burnt to death.'

Soon afterwards I wrote to the Bishop of Salisbury, an Old Shirburnian who was Chairman of the Governing Body, to tell him that I was no longer happy as an Assistant Chaplain at the school, and I had no prospect of promotion. I expected that he might offer me a post as a curate at a town parish in the Salisbury diocese. To my great surprise he offered me the living of Charminster, whose vicar was also chaplain at the Dorset Mental Hospital at Herrison, with about 1,000 patients. I promptly accepted, and notified the Headmaster that I would be leaving Sherborne in July. Shortly before the end of the summer term he summoned me to his office, in order to inform me that he intended to be ordained, and wished it to be known that it was not because he was losing an ordained member of the staff!

I conducted the Commemoration Service in the abbey, as the vicar had no singing voice – he was a friend of mine, as I had helped him by taking Sunday services in churches for which he was responsible.

In the afternoon on the school playing fields I happened to be near Mr Wallace, and could not help overhearing a parent make a complimentary remark to him about the singing voice of the priest that had conducted the abbey service. 'Oh, not bad for an amateur,' was the Headmaster's reply.

In the following two years the Director of School Music, Mr B.J.F. Picton, insisted that I should be invited to conduct the Commemoration Service, an invitation that I gladly accepted.

For several years I acted as Chaplain to the local branch of the Toc H League of Women Helpers. All that I can remember now is (i) talking to a member with a 'problem' over a long period and her sending me letters; (ii) an address I gave on the prayer beginning, 'Teach me, O Lord, to serve Thee as Thou deservest'.

There was no school orchestra in those days, and for concerts by the choral society Mr Picton engaged local professional and amateur players to play the accompaniment. Hardly any boys learnt how to play instruments except the piano, for which ample provision was made in the building erected about 100 yards from the Entrance Gateway. I contributed only one tenor solo at a school concert – the Scottish folk song, *Ca' the yowes*, set to music by Vaughan Williams for unaccompanied voices. A chord was played on the piano, and I sang the opening phrase, and the chorus followed. I thought that it sounded at a higher pitch then usual. Afterwards Mr Picton confirmed my suspicion – the pianist had played a chord of D flat instead of one of B flat, and we all had sung the piece a minor third higher than intended.

Only one other master joined me in singing tenor in the chorus of men and boys, and only very few boys joined us; most teenagers, when their treble voices 'break', become baritones. My enjoyable musical experiences at the school certainly developed my sight-reading ability.

Only four of my Sherborne diaries have survived, for the years 1929, 1933, 1934 and 1936, and they record a few events that I had forgotten, but they have many blank pages, and mainly record some of my engagements.

I attended meetings of the Mathematical Association in London on January 7th and 8th, 1929, and returned to Sherborne on the 16th, presumably on my bicycle (about 110 miles). After an uneventful spring term, when I had a few pupils for 'extra tuition' at 7.30 a.m., on March 28th I cycled 63 miles to meet my father at Winchester, and went with him $37^{1}/_{2}$ miles to find bed and breakfast in Chichester (my first visit there). Next day we cycled only 32 miles along the coast road through Arundel, Worthing and Shoreham to reach Brighton for the night. On Sunday we made a detour to Uckfield, where my sister Doreen was living, having a teaching post at a girls' school there, and returned to Brighton again. On the next day our route was along the Kent coast road through Folkestone, Dover, Sandwich, Ramsgate and Margate, and then inland to Canterbury: after visiting the cathedral we cycled on to Chilham and spent the night at a pub (the Woolpack Inn?). We then returned to our home in East Acton in a leisurely way, spending one night at Seale, and then completing our Easter tour of 334 miles.

During the summer holidays my father and I made another long cycle tour together. We met at Romsey, and spent the first night at Bridport, reaching Okehampton in Devon the next evening. Then we began to enjoy the beautiful scenery of Cornwall, finding bed and breakfast for two nights at Camelford. We visited Truro Cathedral, and spent two nights in Penzance, making an excursion to Land's End, which had not yet been spoilt by commercialisation. After spending a night at Falmouth and two nights at Fowey, we reached Plymouth, where we parted company. I spent nights at Brixham and Sherborne on my way to Sutton Courtenay, near Oxford, where I assisted at the Christ Church camp for London boys for eight days. Then I returned to Brixham to join my family for the remainder of the summer holiday.

No record of my cycling activities during the next two years has survived. On January 6th, 1933, I gave my talk on 'Lewis Carroll – Mathematician' to the AGM of the Mathematical Association, which I had joined as a life member in 1927.

During the following Easter holidays I attended several promenade concerts at the Queen's Hall, conducted by Sir Henry Wood – often with the company of Sherborne boys.

For a few years I acted as the local representative of the Royal Schools of Music, and was responsible for arranging the written and practical examinations that took place in my room at Tantallon. A piano was lent by my neighbours, Mr and Mrs Jarrett. Amongst the distinguished examiners that I had the privilege of entertaining were Sir Arthur Somervell and Dr Thalben Ball. I recollect that Sir Arthur was then an old man on a milk diet, and so unable to enjoy the special dinner that Mrs Pope had prepared for us.

I have no need of diaries to stimulate my recollections of many happy events during my 11 years in Sherborne: I enjoyed my various activities and felt that I was making a con-tribution to the social life of the school and the town.

One autumn term when the Sherborne Operatic Society was

not rehearsing a Gilbert and Sullivan opera, Mr Picton, the school's Director of Music, kept the singers together by conducting rehearsals of a programme of music for Christmastide, for performance at a number of large country mansions near Sherborne, but he resigned when attendances at rehearsals dropped off. It was said that several of the singers disliked the choice of carols, some of which contained Latin words. I was invited to 'step into his shoes', which I gladly did. I continued the rehearsals, and enjoyed the performances with a smaller group of keen singers, the first of which I think was at Milborne Port House. I had had a little experience of conducting prior to this, as Mrs Gadesden, who lived at Holwell Manor, had invited me to conduct a small string orchestra that met at her house every Wednesday evening. It was named the Triad Orchestra, as its members came from three small villages. It already had its name inscribed on a silver trophy, as it had won the competition for small orchestras at the Dorset Choral Association's annual music festival.

Its good fortune continued under my baton – probably because there was no other string orchestra in Dorset to challenge us. Naturally I was sorry to have to give up my musical activities in Sherborne when I became the Vicar of Charminster, and I formed a choral society that entered for the village choir competition at the last pre-war festival of the Dorset Choral Association, which was organised by a group of ladies of leisure. After the war ended these ladies with one exception had lost their enthusiasm for competitive music festivals and would not support the revival of such activities. A new committee and officers had to be found; I offered to act as honorary secretary and treasurer for one year to assist Mrs Bright in this task. With the invaluable support of the Dorset County Council's Director of Music in Schools, Dr Reginald Johnson, we began raising funds by means of two concerts by an 'ad hoc' choir, which he trained and conducted. The first performance was given at Weymouth – Mendelssohn's

Elijah – and the second at Wimborne Minster of excerpts from Bach's *Christmas Oratorio*. As I left Dorset in the next year I have no record of whether this enabled them to revive the competitive festivals.

My last few months in Sherborne, after I had accepted the living of Charminster, were taken up with frequent visits to the Vicarage, making plans for its furnishing. My leaving present from the staff was a fine oak desk, and my father made a large bookcase that covered one wall of the study. My parents let me have their mahogany dining room table and chairs, and in exchange I bought them a smaller set of walnut wood for their smaller dining room in the new house they had built at Waterside, on the cliffs of Torbay. My sister bought the bedroom furniture for the room she occupied as my housekeeper for the first six months and made a present of them on leaving. The remaining furniture was bought from the firm Shepherd and Hedger in Dorchester, including a grandfather clock that needed some repair, costing I think £3. My parents also gave me a second-hand grand piano that they bought at Selfridges for about £30 – it helped to fill the empty space in the large lounge.

So the day arrived when I left Tantallon's two rooms for the large Victorian Vicarage, where we had furnished the whole of the ground floor and three bedrooms on the first floor, leaving four attic rooms empty. My bank account was probably empty too, but I was now independent – and for the first time in my life I had a telephone in my study – Dorchester 477.

ENVOI

On the thirty-third anniversary of my birth on July 22nd, 1938, the Sherborne Madrigal Club gave a farewell recital in the upper room of the Music School to an audience of invited friends. This was the programme:

Sing we and chant it – Morley
On the plains, fairy trains – Weelkes
The silver swan – Gibbons
Ave verum corpus (motet) – Byrd
My bonny lass she smileth – Morley
Thus saith my Cloris – Wilbye
Wilt thou unkind thus reave me? – Dowland
Fire, fire, my heart – Morley
Lullaby, my sweet little baby – Byrd
Flora gave me fairest flowers – Wilbye
In going to my lonely bed – Edwards

7

Charminster

My Induction Service as Vicar of Charminster in the late summer of 1938 was attended by parishioners and men and women friends from Sherborne, and Gerald Ellison, who was then Chaplain to the Bishop of Winchester. As I was also responsible for morning and evening services on Sundays at Herrison Hospital, I continued my predecessor's practice of employing a diocesan lay reader for one of these services – for which the fee then was 10s per service – and I also had the assistance of Mr H.J. Ford, the Headmaster of Charminster Church of England School, who was also a parochial lay reader.

I greatly enjoyed conducting these services, and was always exhilarated by the final one each Sunday – Evensong in the beautiful church at Charminster. I still have a mental picture of the first Evensong, when I found that the singing by the small choir was augmented by a bevy of maidens and matrons sitting in the front pew.

My fiancée, Miss Phyllis May Perrett, would travel by bus from Sherborne each Saturday and stay at a hotel in Dorchester, until kind friends in the village offered her hospitality, and then return to Sherborne on Sunday evening. The church organist was Mr Kibbey, who lived in Dorchester; Mrs Florence Bankes – the grand old lady who occupied Wolfeton House – accompanied the hymns at the afternoon children's service, and Mrs Trivett was the chapel organist at Herrison Hospital.

I compiled only two sermons each week for delivery in the parish church, and in a modified form at the hospital chapel, making copious notes for reading, as I could never trust myself to preach extempore addresses to adults, although my talk to children on Sunday afternoons and my weekly 'lessons' to the senior class at the school were prepared only mentally.

All went smoothly according to plan for several months, until the outbreak of World War II on Sunday, September 3rd, when a messenger brought the news just before I began my sermon. The only immediate effect that this had on me was that the plans for my wedding at Shipley later in September had to be changed. The Revd J.C. Barker was to have been my best man, but he felt he could not leave his parish in Kent at a time when bombs might begin to fall, and so Geoffrey, Phyllis's brother, took his place. Phyllis also had to find a deputy bridesmaid living in Shipley for our wedding on September 26th, taken by her father, the Revd W.J. Perrett, in his parish church at Shipley. We had a brief honeymoon in the Lake District, spending two nights at the St Martin's hotel, Ambleside, one night at Chester, and then headed south. On arriving at Stroud we found that all the hotels had been commandeered by the military authorities and we eventually found bed and breakfast at a farm house, where conditions were primitive. It happened to be the night when National Registration numbers were issued, so that we appear to have been residents in Gloucestershire. We reached Charminster in time to resume normal duties on Sunday.

Very soon the village was denuded of all its middle-aged men. Captain Bennett was in charge of the local civil defence organisation, but on his death a few weeks later, I became the Head Warden, whilst Phyllis was in charge of the Red Cross Emergency Unit, and Mr H.J. Ford captained the Local Defence Volunteers, later called the Home Guard. Phyllis made and I put up black-out curtains to the clerestory windows in the church, so that evening services continued, with smaller congregations. During one National Savings Week films were shown in the church, and I well remember the sight of a plane zooming out through the Norman chancel arch.

One evening Phyllis and I were in Dorchester in a church rehearsing Handel's *Judas Maccabaeus* when the air-raid sirens sounded. I continued conducting and Phyllis continued playing the organ accompaniment. We heard enemy planes flying overhead, but when we returned to Charminster about an hour later, all was quiet and peaceful. Early the next morning the Deputy Head Warden called at the Vicarage to tell me that during the night many incendiary bombs had fallen on the north end of the village; one council house had been set on fire (the bomb landed by the bedside of a choirboy) but the fire had soon been put out by a warden using a stirrup pump. A haystack had been set on fire, and bombs falling on thatch-roofed cottages had been seen to bounce off. After the war my wife and I both received Defence Medals – we had never been in action, but simply organised and trained personnel.

Shortly before World War II Doreen took a post at the English College in Buenos Aires, but when war broke out she returned to England via Canada at a time when many lives were being lost, due to U-boat activity.

She joined the Enigma team at Bletchley Park, about which she was sworn to secrecy, and I do not even know whether she met Alan Turing personally. After the war she settled in Shrewsbury, and bought a picturesque old house, 10 St Almund's Square, and taught in several girls' schools in the neighbourhood – Acton Reynold is the only name I can remember. All went well until our mother's last illness, when Doreen had 'retired' and wished to return to our home at Waterside, Paignton, in order to nurse my mother. But my father and I did not think this was a good idea, as Doreen was temperamentally unlikely to bring comfort and solace to her mother in her old age.

My mother was left a legacy of £2,000 by Cousin Florrie, a distant relative of my father; this covered the expense almost to a penny of my mother's residence at nursing homes in Paignton. Shortly after my mother's death my father sold 12 Waterside Road and went to live at boarding houses in Paignton, and died in Paignton Hospital after a stroke at the age of 90 years.

Soon after Phyllis had taken up residence at the Vicarage, Mr Kibbey resigned, and a little later, Mrs Bankes gave up playing for the children's services; I have an idea that she was annoyed by the organ blower dozing off during my talk, and the result was a dying wail from the organ when she tried to play over the hymn tune. The story may be mythical, but the Parochial Church Council met the cost of installing an electric blower when Phyllis became the honorary church organist. Church funds could easily afford this, and they later met the cost of installing electric heaters under the pews to supplement the heat from a large old-fashioned stove that was relit each Saturday night. Money collected during services mounted, due to generous contributions from a number of well-to-do residents – retired Admirals, Colonels, etc. I had control of the Vicar's Discretionary Fund, financed solely by the offerings by visitors to the church.

I also organised a Christmas Club with the aid of a number of voluntary collectors, who visited members of the club each week and entered the amount they contributed on a card, and brought the cash to me for deposit in a Savings Bank account, thus earning interest. Some shops in Dorchester would accept the cards as payment for goods whose value exceeded the amount contributed by the member, and send them to me for reimbursement. There was a small post office not far from the bridge over the river Cerne near the church, which sold little else but confectionery, and there was a small shop at the north end of the village. Consequently we all had to take our ration books to the shops in Dorchester once a week.

In January 1939 I became the Honorary Secretary and Treasurer of the Dorset Voluntary Schools Association, whose main function was to allocate grants to the managers of Church schools in the county for the maintenance of old buildings that needed repair, using funds provided by the Salisbury diocese and by national educational charities. A committee met regularly to allocate the grants, and I made a quarterly report to the Diocesan Council of Education. This necessitated frequent visits to Salisbury, as I was also on the Diocesan Board of Finance and attended the annual Diocesan Conference, where I once made a speech. I have described these activities in my booklet entitled *Dorchester in the 20th Century*.

Phyllis joined the local branches of the Mothers' Union and the Women's Institute, and organised a working party that met each week at the Vicarage to make garments for soldiers and sailors and needy civilians. Parochial engagements in the evenings were frequent – committee meetings of the Parochial Church Council, School Managers, Parish Hall Managers, choir practices and rehearsals of the Choral Society, concerts and quizzes in aid of various good causes.

I had little spare time to 'Dig for Victory', but managed the large garden, as the gardener who had begun to assist me soon retired. I kept about a dozen hens in a corner of the garden where there was a wooden shed for roosting and boxes for egg-laying. I collected the egg ration coupons from relatives and neighbours, and obtained in exchange 'balancer meal', which, mixed with cooked vegetable-refuse, formed a nourishing diet for the poultry, so that they produced plenty of eggs – enough for our needs and our neighbours'; in the end I had a surplus for sale to the Egg Marketing Board in Dorchester.

I allowed a neighbour whose house adjoined the garden on the far side of Vicarage Lane to use part of the vegetable plot, whilst the fruit trees produced an abundance of cooking and dessert apples, and the gooseberry bushes provided over 200 pounds of fruit one year – the surplus being sold to Herrison Hospital.

I was told that a former vicar, who was also the Archdeacon of Dorset, had bought a part of a field for the benefit of his daughter, who rode horses, and that a subsequent incumbent had made it into a garden, surrounded by perennial hedges, with grass lawns and pathways, and had planted a wide variety of fruit trees, leaving a huge old oak tree to dominate the far end of the garden. Fortunately for me the fruit trees had reached the stage when they needed little pruning, and a decrepit old mulberry tree yielded luscious fruit each year. The grass in the churchyard was scythed regularly before the war, but no one was available for this job during the war years, and the experiment was made of tethering a white nanny goat in a different area each day. This soon proved to be a failure, as more grass was trampled on than eaten, and the PCC made a present of the goat to my wife. She let it feed in the hedgerows of Vicarage Lane, and milked it after it had produced two kids that were sold. Nanny became a pet, and eventually died of old age.

When I became Vicar of Charminster my predecessor, Canon D.F. Slemeck, gave me a small book containing the names of the occupants of every house in the village, to which he paid an annual visit. A weakness of my ministry was that I did not follow his example, and only visited homes when circumstances necessitated it. There were several such occasions during the war years, when a family lost a son in the fighting forces. One incident remains in my mind when Captain and Mrs Lee Norman's son was trained as a pilot in the Royal Air Force, but lost his life when he crashed his plane on his first solo flight. I was often at a loss as to what to say to the mourners, as I could not use the phrases often employed by clergymen, to the effect that separation was only temporary, as they would be reunited with their loved ones in the next world.

A year or so after the war ended, about 12 new names were added to the memorial cross in the churchyard commemorating a larger number of young men who had died during World War I. There was one regrettable dispute as to whether the name of the son-in-law of Captain and Mrs Leschallas should be carved on the War Memorial: he had died whilst serving with the British Army of Occupation in Germany several months after hostilities had ended, and the cause of death was over-indulgence in alcohol. He had not been a resident in Charminster, but had no fixed abode after his marriage. The War Memorial Committee was divided in its opinion, and many shared my view that he did not deserve commemoration together with those who had sacrificed their lives whilst fighting for their King and Country. In the end it was decided that as he had been a member of the Regular Army before the war, his name should be commemorated somewhere, and the only possibility was in Charminster.

Another committee was formed after the war had ended in order to make arrangements for the 'welcome home' of those who survived. Funds were collected to finance a series of dinners in the parish hall, to be attended by the returning men and a few representatives of those who had remained at home. At least three such dinners were held over a period of several months, and at the final event there were only about four men to be the guests. None of them appeared – presumably because they did not want a fuss to be made of them so long after the war had ended, and the dinner was eaten by some members of the organising committee.

Throughout the war various kinds of entertainment had taken place in the parish hall, except during a short period when it was used by the military authorities. The Women's

Institute continued to give dramatic and musical evenings, and there were competitive quizzes between various groups, such as the REME soldiers living in huts in the field adjoining the Vicarage garden against a group of volunteers from the village. I remember one 'concert' given by professional actors and actresses in a company that toured Great Britain giving performances to boost morale. After the war activities gradually returned to pre-war level: a dramatic society was formed and staged a performance of one of Priestley's plays, and I wrote one-act comedies in which I appeared with men and women villagers. With the aid of the headmaster and staff of the school, scenes that I selected from Dickens' *A Christmas Carol* were enacted on the small stage before full houses in the hall, and it could seat about 100 people.

A group of men gave a 'variety show', no programme of which has survived; all I can recollect is that it included a male-voice trio, for which I arranged some well-known songs. This proved to be so popular that we gave performances in the halls of three neighbouring villages. At one there was only a platform in lieu of a stage, and at another the piano was unplayable and so all our vocal items had to be sung without accompaniment. All of us enjoyed these activities enormously.

The last venture of this kind for which I was responsible was a staged version of scenes from *Alice in Wonderland*, to be performed by schoolchildren. The script consisted entirely of words that Lewis Carroll put into the mouths of the human and animal speakers in Wonderland. I set to music some of the amusing verses from the book, and the percussion band of the infants class performed the *Wonderland March*, which opened the performance. Three girls of different sizes impersonated Alice: a five-year-old was the tiny Alice, a ten-year-old was the normal Alice who endured transformations of height, whilst Doris Kendall, a former pupil at the school, now 17 years old, made an attractive tall Alice. The changes of size were made during short black-out periods. At the last moment the boy who should have been the Mock Turtle was taken ill, and so I took over the part, wearing a dustbin lid as my carapace. This caused headlines in the local papers: CANON TURNS TURTLE.

Another post-war innovation was made by a new resident with a cine-camera, who took films of events such as the summer fair at Brooklands, the home of Mr and Mrs K.P. Druce. He also took shots of buildings and views of the village from the top of the church tower. He filmed a procession in the school playground of the children in their *Alice in Wonderland* costumes. One parishioner, who lived in a small house at the north-west corner of the churchyard, failed to recognise herself when she appeared on the screen in the parish hall, exclaiming, 'That's not me, is it?' Naturally these cinema shows attracted large audiences of people wanting to see if they appeared in any of the films. The last showing in my time was in Coronation Year, 1953, and I wonder what has happened to them now in the twenty-first century, as they should be of historic interest.

I must now put the clock back again – to the month when World War II began. A few days before war was declared a party of about 50 schoolgirls and two teachers were evacuated from London, and the Chairman of the Parish Council had to find billets for them in the village. I was surprised and delighted to learn that they were from the Haberdashers' Aske's Girls' School in Acton. I offered them the use of the four empty attic rooms at the Vicarage as temporary classrooms, the walls of which they redecorated. So when I returned with my wife early in September, she found a family of 50 girls occupying the house and garden each day. This lasted only a short time, as the evacuees returned to London shortly after Christmas. Before they left they gave a carol service in the church, when Phyllis and I made the acquaintance of two carols from Czechoslovakia, which we immediately added to our repertoire.

Later on I began composing Anglican chants, hymn tunes and carols. A carol party toured the village each year, collecting money for some good cause, and for the first time I entered one of the village pubs at the invitation of the owner to sing inside instead of in the cold outside. One year a choirboy, Edwin Hawker, went carol singing on his own, and I was amused and flattered to hear that he had sung my tune for the carol *Waken, Christian Children*. I introduced a few of my chants for the canticles and psalms, which met with the approval of the church choir, and when I discovered that the organists at some neighbouring churches were using chants that they had composed, I had the idea of publishing a book of new chants. I wrote a letter to the editor of the *Sarum Gazette*, asking him to publish a notice inviting organists throughout the diocese to send me copies of the chants they had composed. Seven musicians formed a panel of adjudicators – including Dr Ley, who had moved from Christ Church, Oxford, to become organist at Eton College, and Dr Reginald Johnson, the Dorset County Music Director for schools – and they were asked to put the chants submitted into four categories: A, the best ones; B, reasonably good; C, not very distinguished but ordinary; D, unusable. I submitted many of my own compositions of single and double chants anonymously. To my surprise and joy, most of those placed in category A were my own. With this backing of seven church musicians I compiled *The Charminster Chant Book*, a mixture of 63 new and old chants by Tudor and Victorian composers – Tallis, Goss, Elvey, Wesley and co. The latter were used mainly to form sets of chants suitable for the Te Deum; new chants by other composers were indicated by their initials, and mine were left anonymous; six chants were printed together as being suitable for the Venite, Benedictus, Jubilate, Nunc Dimittis, and the Magnificat or Cantate and the Deus

Misereatur. The last four pages had new chants for particular psalms, and well-known chants printed with versions with descants. Two editions were needed, the proceeds going to Church school funds in each parish in the Salisbury diocese. I think each body of managers received 15s! For the same purpose I compiled *The Lewis Carroll Puzzle Book* – a mixture of his problems (doublets, etc.) and quizzes and crossword puzzles that I had invented.

Two afternoons each week were spent in visits to Herrison Hospital. On arrival I would go to the office to obtain information about new arrivals in the male and female admission wards before visiting them. Most of the wards housed permanent patients to whom I could not give any help, but I hope that my chats with the nurses helped to boost their morale and show appreciation of their self-sacrificial work.

When I was an undergraduate I made the acquaintance of the Chaplain at Lancaster Mental Hospital, and asked him whether I could visit it with him. He kindly took me round some of the male wards one afternoon; I still have vivid recollections of two experiences there.

We entered a large ward which was completely empty except for a buxom nurse sitting on a chair, with a group of about a dozen men sitting on the floor around her. She was mending some garments, and as soon as we entered she jumped up, scattering a box of buttons around her. I expected that pandemonium would break out, but instead the men scrambled quietly retrieving the buttons. That incident taught me several lessons, amongst which was the fact that mental hospitals, like other kinds of hospitals, are Christian institutions, where devoted men and women nurses spend their lives caring for those in trouble of mind or body – a truly Christian vocation. These patients too wished to help the nurse, and were on friendly terms with her.

The second incident was very different: a patient asked me whether I would shortly be going to London. I replied that I might well be in London before long. He then told me that his name was (something like) Captain George William Henry Brown, and that the numerical value of it (calculated by giving each letter of the alphabet a value) was the same as 'He shall rule the nation with a rod of iron', and so it was his destiny to be the King of England. Would I please go and tell King George V that he had no right to be King? I replied that I doubted whether I should meet King George V, but if I ever did, I would pass on the message. I learnt that most patients behaved quietly, were on good terms with the staff, and that many suffered from delusions as the result of an emotional shock, such as the sudden death of a loved one.

In consequence when the Bishop of Salisbury invited me to become Chaplain at the Dorset mental hospital, I had no hesitation in accepting the offer. My most unpleasant experience was when a parishioner, who had spent a period in the hospital, was discharged and returned home, but came to the Vicarage one night to complain about the treatment he had received, and thought I was responsible for what he had endured.

I remember the name of one patient – Minnie Poulter – who always sent me a picture postcard of the places she had visited on a coach tour for patients. Private patients lived at Herrison House in their own bedrooms at night, and in comfortable lounges by day. I made the acquaintance of a grand old lady who thought that she was Queen Victoria, and dressed and looked like her. I had conversations with an epileptic man, and sometimes spent a few minutes playing snooker with him. With several of the medical staff – doctors, matrons, sisters and nurses – and some of the administrative staff, I formed friendships, and was invited to be a godfather to the son of a Chief Administrator, Mr Ailwyn Thacker, who left to take up a similar post in Suffolk. My wife and I frequently stayed with them in Woodbridge when on holiday. Their son has been Vicar of Hammersmith for many years.

The hospital chapel was full each Sunday for the two services that I conducted – Matins or Holy Communion in the morning and Evensong in the evening, with a small choir of nurses to lead the singing. On one occasion a Hammond electronic organ was hired, so that my wife could accompany a performance of an oratorio in the large main hall, which was used for other forms of entertainment, such as the annual performance of a pantomime given by the staff who displayed vocal and dramatic talents, and a chorus of 'glamour girls'. Most of the staff lived on the premises, but some of the male nurses were married men with homes in the village. I was indebted to the kitchen staff for a regular supply of vegetable-waste that I used to cook and feed to my poultry. During the war we were glad to be able to buy honey at a shilling per pot from the occupant of a cottage on the hospital estate.

My activities as Hospital Chaplain for 15 years did not produce any kind of strain; mental hospitals are not full of raving lunatics, as some people may imagine, but places where members of the staff are able to express in a practical way their Christian desire to help those in need of care. When I left, the governing body gave me a parting present and a letter of thanks for my services. When asked what we would like as a parting gift from the parishioners, we said we would like a watercolour of the exterior of Charminster church. Our wish was granted, and the accompanying framed list of the names of 200 donors to the fund that paid for it shows how many friends we had in Charminster.

Much of the time that I spent in my study each day was concerned with the Church of England primary schools in Dorset, and the three proposed 'special agreement' secondary schools in Wyke Regis (Weymouth), Puddletown and Sherborne. As Honorary Treasurer of the Dorset Voluntary Schools Association, I found in the old accounts book that a few schools had deposited some funds with the DVSA for safe keeping, which had been forgotten. I arranged for these to be repaid. Requests for grants towards the cost of repairs of school buildings were considered by a committee that met regularly and allocated funds provided by the Salisbury Council of Education and the Board of Finance, and educational charities such as Bettons. I became the diocesan representative on the Dorset County Education Committee, which wished to ensure that the Agreed Syllabus of Religious Instruction was being properly used in all of its secondary modern schools; so during one year I and a Free Church colleague acted as 'inspectors'. In 1943 I devised a contributory scheme, whereby the Managers of Dorset primary schools could obtain 'Aided Status' under the forthcoming Education Act 1944, by payment of a fixed annual amount to the diocesan Board of Finance; in return the board would meet the whole cost of repairs and improvements demanded by the 1944 Act. The scheme was approved by the Diocesan Council of Education and the Ministry of Education, which adopted it for use in all English dioceses, under the title of 'The Barchester Scheme'.

The fixed payment under the Barchester Scheme depended upon the size of the school, which was based on the insured value of the buildings and the average number of children enrolled; as a result 99 Church schools in Dorset acquired Aided Status. This meant that the managers appointed the head teacher and the assistant staff, and a CE syllabus of religious education was used in the classrooms.

In recognition of my work for religious education in the diocese of Salisbury, in 1951 the Bishop appointed me to be an Honorary Canon of the cathedral, and Prebendary of Netherbury in Ecclesia. I had to preach in the cathedral once a year, and had done so only twice, when in 1953 I left the diocese and became a Canon Emeritus.

After the evacuees had left Charminster at the end of 1939

and returned to London, our four attic rooms were commandeered by the military authorities for use as billets for soldiers. We were paid 2d per night per man. Meanwhile huts were being built in the field next to the Vicarage garden, where a large REME base was established. We were soon on friendly terms with the Commandant, but the soldiers played no part in the social life of the village.

When our attics were no longer needed as billets, the local council took them over in order to house families bombed out of their London homes. After the war was over and the rooms were derequisitioned, the rector of a Dorset village told me that his daughter had married an ex-officer who had obtained a post at Dorchester Grammar School, and they needed accommodation for themselves and their three young children, the youngest of whom was a baby boy. So Mr and Mrs Sewell furnished the rooms, and the family was welcomed as residents.

The inhabitants of Charminster could be divided into two distinct classes: the upper class of retired well-to-do Army and Navy officers and prosperous land-owning farmers, and the working class with jobs at Herrison Hospital or in Dorchester, or running public houses or small shops. The Sewells were the first representatives of the professional classes (except the headmaster of the school) to reside in the village. Mr Sewell was particularly welcome, as he was a staunch member of the church and joined in the social activities; he and Mr Ford formed a male voice trio that contributed to entertainments in the parish hall and neighbouring villages. Eventually Mr Sewell purchased some derelict property on glebe land near the church, renovated it and moved into it The last occupants of the attic rooms were a widow, Mrs Edwards, and her son.

After derequisitioning we did not receive rent from the residents, but hoped that they would give us some help in the house and garden. This amicable arrangement proved satisfactory in some cases but not in others.

In 1938 there was an electric cooker in the kitchen but no provision for heating the room, and I cannot recollect what arrangements there were for washing, drying and ironing the laundry. There were open fires in the study and lounge, and an anthracite-burning stove heated the dining room. Some time after the war had ended, diocesan funds paid for the installation of an Aga cooker in the kitchen, which provided not only ovens for cooking and warmth for the room, but also hot water for the taps in the scullery and bathroom. The Board of Finance fixed an annual charge to repay the cost over a period of years; I think we had paid three or four instalments before we left.

Most of the boundary of the garden surrounding the Vicarage was old stone walling, several sections of which I rebuilt from time to time. The Vicarage building was kept in repair and redecorated externally by a diocesan body that levied an annual payment from the incumbent.

Our grand piano was played not only by Phyllis, but also by a parishioner without access to an instrument. He seemed keen to produce as much sound as he could, in contrast to Phyllis's more delicate playing. Occasional gramophone recitals were given: a REME soldier brought his records of a modern piano concerto to supplement my own classical records.

During World War II the instrumental and choral festivals organised by the Dorset Choral Association naturally lapsed. After the war the previous organisers no longer wished to promote competitive festivals, and only one member of the pre-war committee was willing to revive the association's activities. So I stepped into the breach and volunteered to co-operate with her, undertaking the job of honorary secretary. Together with Dr R. Johnson, the organiser of music in schools for the Dorset County Council Education Committee, we formed a choir, which rehearsed Bach's *Christmas Oratorio*, and he conducted a performance in Wimborne Minster, thereby raising funds. He also rehearsed Mendelssohn's *Elijah*, the performance of which in Weymouth was even more profitable. Then I was able to hand over to a new committee and honorary secretary and treasurer before I left Charminster.

The small church choir was able to sing an occasional anthem from the *Church Anthem Book*, and its adult members formed the nucleus of a choral society capable of singing a simple cantata, such as *The Last Supper* by Eric Thiman. My wife's assistance as organ accompanist was invaluable.

After the war when petrol became more plentiful, we could visit friends in nearby villages and spend an evening singing madrigals. In the diocese I became Chairman of the Diocesan Music Committee, and was responsible for organising choir festivals in rural deaneries and in the cathedral, with the co-operation of David Willcocks, the cathedral organist. I can still visualise a festival in the cathedral attended by hundreds of choristers from Wiltshire and Dorset. I ventured to conduct a choir festival in a Wiltshire rural deanery, and David Willcocks came to conduct a similar event in Dorchester.

In 1953 we recommended some anthems by Thomas Weelkes as suitable for performance during Coronation year.

The Workers' Educational Association invited me to give three series of lecture-recitals in Dorset villages. My wife and I enjoyed our weekly visits to Corfe Castle, Moreton and Melplash, where my talks or classical music were illustrated by gramophone records, songs and the piano. I forget what I was paid for this amateur enterprise, but the fees would hardly justify my regarding myself as a professional musician.

In 1953 Bishop George Bell, Bishop of Chichester, was Chairman of the Governors of Bishop Otter College, and it was he who confirmed my appointment as Chaplain and mathematical lecturer at the college from September of that year.

When approaching his retirement, the Headmaster of

Sherborne School accepted the living of Moreton, a truly rural parish in the Rural Deanery of Dorchester, where most of the incumbents were elderly clergymen, including four Canons and an Archdeacon. The Bishop of Salisbury invited me to become the next Rural Dean, and I served in this office during the last six months of my 22 years as a priest in the diocese, and assisted the Archdeacon of Sherborne at two Inductions. I already knew most of the 15 parishes in and around Dorchester, through visiting their Church schools as a Diocesan Inspector, and it would be my duty to see that the Diocesan Syllabus was properly taught by the new Rector and the staff of Moreton CE School, and to help and advise about any pastoral problems that arose, as he had no previous experience of life in a country parish. His acceptance of a prestigious post in the diocese of Exeter, however, saved him from having to face any such problems.

Happy memories of 15 busy years spent in the heart of Thomas Hardy country, in the service of all sorts and conditions of men, women and children, are suffused with a sense of gratitude to them for their constant courtesy and friendliness. Amongst my many friends in the parish and diocese, I remember especially the Matron and nurses, several from the occupied countries of Eastern Europe, the medical and administrative staff of Herrison Hospital, who devoted their lives to the welfare of 1,000 mentally ill patients.

8

Chichester

In the spring of 1953 I was one of the two clergymen interviewed for the post of Chaplain at Bishop Otter College, for which I was told over 40 parish priests had applied. Phyllis and I stayed at a hotel in the centre of Chichester, and were invited in the evening to a coffee party at the college, where we met the principal and several of the lecturers.

On the next morning I was interviewed by Miss K.M.E. Murray and the Archdeacon of Chichester in lieu of the Bishop of Chichester, Dr G.K.A. Bell, and I was delighted to learn that they recommended me for the post that had been temporarily filled by Canon Lowther Clarke. We were invited to stay at the Palace with Dr and Mrs Bell, but now I have no recollection of our conversation. The Bishop did not appear at breakfast next day, as he had had an attack of asthma, and I was invited to conduct Matins in the chapel. Unfortunately I read the psalms for the wrong day, and apologised to Mrs Bell when I discovered my mistake. She replied to the effect that she did not mind, as the psalms I had read were amongst her favourites.

The residence for the Chaplain was a mile away from the impressive Victorian-Gothic buildings of Bishop Otter College. The fine Georgian house, 6 North Pallant, in the heart of Chichester, was also used as a hostel for 16 women students, with the Chaplain's wife as Warden. My duties were not onerous, involving the organisation of choral morning and evening services in the chapel on weekdays, and conducting an early Celebration on Sundays. Most of the short daily services were conducted by the Principal or students, but at the full Evensongs on Wednesdays I would give an occasional sermon or invite one of the canons of the cathedral or local parish priests to occupy the pulpit.

All students took a basic divinity course, to which I contributed a series of lectures on the history of the Christian Church, and the history of the Book of Common Prayer. Altogether there were 220 women students taking the two-year course for the Teacher's Certificate, and there was a small group of students, including one young man, taking a one-year supplementary course in divinity.

A new challenge awaited me as the sole lecturer in mathematics; I was responsible for the two-year course in basic mathematics for students preparing to teach in junior and secondary schools. Only four students had chosen mathematics as their main subject, the others available being English literature, physical education, art, history, geography, biology, French and a number of crafts – weaving, pottery, needlecraft – and horticulture. Secondary students chose two of these main subjects and the others chose one.

The course included topics comparable to those in an A-level syllabus, concluding with an examination set in collaboration with the external examiner from Reading University.

The general standard of entrants was high, as the Principal could select from many more candidates than the college could accept, but comparatively few had obtained an O-level pass in mathematics, and some had done little or no mathematics for more than four years, and feared the prospect of teaching the subject to young children. Remedial work was never mentioned, but the basic course had to stimulate the interest of all, whilst helping the weakest without being tedious to those keen to learn the techniques required in the classroom.

Every teacher is expected to achieve 100 per cent accuracy when adding up marks, keeping attendance registers, working out averages and percentages, handling dinner money, etc., and so there was a natural incentive to become competent in such simple arithmetical tasks. For the guidance of lecturers and students there were books like Monteith's *The Teaching of Arithmetic in Primary Schools*, and a stimulating book by Mrs L.D. Adams on the wide variety of mathematical activities possible in a primary school. The style and contents of textbooks for young children were changing, and in secondary schools the syllabus was rapidly widening. Although one followed the Board of Education's current *Handbook of Suggestions for Teachers*, which contained a short final chapter on mathematics, advising that 'a course should not be on rigid lines', and that 'methods should be standardised in a group of Primary Schools contributory to a Senior School', one felt that a college course of 60 lectures in two years (one per week) could hardly equip adequately the future teachers. How much should they be told about the recent researches of Piaget into the child's conception of number, of space, of geometry, etc?

The course for students in the secondary group included many topics in the course for the junior group, as it was expected that most of them would teach only the less bright children in the 11–13 age group. For those with higher aspirations, there were books and the series of reports prepared for the Mathematical Association by panels of experienced teachers on the teaching of arithmetic, algebra, geometry, etc., covering the topics taught in schools prior to 1950, mainly to the more able pupils.

The 1932 arithmetic report had a long section on a variety of methods for the multiplication and division of decimals, recommending that teachers should be acquainted with them all. 'SOME BRIEF REMARKS on the FIRST FOUR RULES' of addition, subtraction, multiplication and division of whole numbers, reminds one of the topics studied by the Mock Turtle at his day-school in the sea: 'Ambition, Distraction, Uglification and Derision'. The 'shop method' of subtraction was recommended and illustrated, though teachers were warned against trying to alter the mental habits of those using 'decomposition' or 'equal additions' methods. 'Inverse addition' is the official title of the 'shop method', and naturally all teachers should understand all three methods, and be able to use them and demonstrate them to pupils. (We were not informed by Lewis Carroll which method Alice tried to use when the Red Queen tested her ability to do 'Subtraction' by asking her to 'Take nine from eight'. 'Nine from eight I can't, you know', Alice replied very readily. What would the Red Queen have said, if Alice had replied, 'Minus one'?)

The official view then was that mathematics in the elementary school had three main purposes: (i) to help the child to form clear ideas about number, time and space; (ii) to make the more useful of these ideas firm and precise in his mind through practice in the appropriate calculations; (iii) to enable him to apply the resulting mechanical skill intelligently, speedily and accurately in the solution of everyday problems. The emphasis was on the purely utilitarian aspects of the subject, but whatever the defects of the basic course I devised, an attempt was made to arouse interest in its intellectual and aesthetic aspects. At the end of the course the external examiner from Reading University would visit the college, and see my assessments of the capability of each student to teach mathematics; many of them had found unexpected success in the classroom when on teaching practice, and had gained in confidence when under the expert supervision of an education lecturer. In theory the external examiner could decide that an incompetent student should have her Teacher's Certificate endorsed with a warning to future employers about her mathematical weakness, but no woman student ever suffered this indignity.

Each student would have on display the visual aids made for teaching practice and any charts, models or apparatus made during the course, and these formed a talking point with the examiner for all the students, some of whom were selected by me to have a personal interview, but none of those chosen for this honour knew whether they were representing the best, average or weaker potentialities. The patterns and colours and toys on display certainly showed that mathematics need not be a dull 'dry-as-dust' subject, and that simple games and recreations had their educational value. Many of the visual aids were artistic as well as useful, though occasionally too ambitious; a chart of shapes, displayed in an infants' classroom on teaching practice, showed a large orange coloured circle labelled SPHERE (probably intended to represent the Sun), and a regular shape with six equal sides labelled SEXAGON.

A young lady of 17 summers once told me that she knew the meaning of 'ratio', and answered correctly the question: A father is 30 years old, and his son is 6 years old; what is the ratio of the father's age to the son's age?' (Answer: the father is five times as old as his son – a ratio of 5 : 1.) When asked: 'And what will the ratio become in six years' time?' she replied, 'The same, of course.' When shown that the ratio would be 3 : 1, she was incredulous, and thought that a mistake in calculation had been made, even when I pointed out that the difference between their ages (24 years) was unchanging, but the ratio of the ages changed every year. When the father was 48, the son would be 24, a ratio of 2 : 1, and if the father reached 72, the ratio would be $1^{1}/_{2}$: 1, and as the years went by the ratio would diminish, getting closer to 1 : 1. She replied, 'Then they would end up being the same age!'

During the first three years everything went smoothly, and in 1956 Mr A.P. Rollett, HMI, suggested that the college should have a one-year supplementary course in mathematics for teachers, adding that he could find the additional lecturers that would be needed: my wife, and a Mr Sparling. When the college authorities had agreed, I became a senior lecturer and signed the current form of agreement, under which lecturers retired at 60 years of age. I was then 53 years old, and my five-year period as Chaplain was due to expire the next year, but Bishop Bell asked me to continue in that office indefinitely. A few years later, just before he retired, the Bishop enquired whether I would be interested in succeeding the Archdeacon of Lewes as the Chichester Diocesan Director of Religious Education, as I had served for seven years on the Council of Education and for three years had been the Diocesan Inspector of Church Schools in the Archdeaconry of Chichester; he quite understood my view that our work in a training college was more congenial.

The supplementary course in mathematics opened in 1957 with 12 teachers living in the neighbourhood of Chichester who attended lectures that I shared with my wife and Mr H.P. Sparling, a grand old bachelor of 69 years who had spent most of his life at Rugby School. He greatly enjoyed this new kind of work with teachers, most of whom were in their forties, some of whom had taken a short post-war course of training and wished to improve their knowledge of secondary school mathematics and their qualifications for teaching the subject. After one year Mr Sparling died suddenly, leaving his mathematical library to the college.

By 1957 rapid strides forward were being made in the design of electronic computers, and so the supplementary course included visits to the National Physical Laboratory, where Deuce was now in operation, and we were able to see how rapidly it performed calculations using some ready-made programmes.

When attending the Mathematical Association's Annual Conference at Manchester, I was able to contact the author of *Faster than Thought* and to see the high-speed machines made by Ferranti that were used at the university. From the information gained I was able to produce for *Mathematical Pie* a film strip describing the history of mechanical calculators from the time of Pascal onwards.

Visits were paid to several computer centres in London, and the one at Southampton University where a programme for factorising numbers quickly revealed a succession of prime numbers, which was useful in a project for investigating Goldbach's Conjecture that every even number is the sum of two prime numbers. We discovered that the number of ways in which an even number could be expressed as the sum of two primes was related to the number of its small prime factors. For example, numbers that are multiples of $30 = 2 \times 3 \times 5$ can be expressed as the sum of two primes in more ways than the even numbers in their neighbourhood.

We visited the Cowley motor works, the HMV factory at Hayes and other industrial centres to learn about their dependence upon the co-operation between mathematicians, statisticians and scientists.

One of the teachers, who had been the art specialist at a secondary modern school, used his talents to paint original designs based upon mathematical curves and shapes. He found that an interesting pattern could be made by representing the sequence of natural numbers in the binary scale by columns of white squares for zeros and black squares for ones. Over 70 teachers took the course during seven years, and several of them found posts as heads of the mathematical departments in secondary modern schools, and one (who had other strings to his bow) has now been on the staff of Sheffield University for some years.

From 1957 onwards the number of entrants to the college wishing to take mathematics as a main course increased rapidly, partly due to the fact that the college was expanding. New hostels were replacing the old dormitories, some of which became lecture rooms. A chapel to seat 400 was built, and the old chapel was transformed into a library after its stained glass windows had been removed. The advent of the three-year training course, the arrival of men students, and the transformation of the physical education main course into a 'wing' for specialists, changed the balance between the main courses considerably. By 1963 English was still the most popular main subject, and mathematics had become the second most popular.

I have pleasant memories of regular visits to meetings of the Chichester Diocesan Council of Education at Hove, taking the Principal, Miss K.M.E. Murray, with me in my car, and of annual visits to CE schools in the Archdeaconry of Chichester. At one of these I found that a local retired priest had given a course of six Lenten addresses based upon *Alice in Wonderland*, culminating in Holy Week with an adaptation of the Trial of the Knave of Hearts as illustrating the Day of Judgment.

The bachelor Archdeacon of Chichester took a great interest in the affairs of the college. His black Labrador dog was frequently to be seen in the grounds. When men students arrived they staged a sketch at a variety concert, in which the Principal's bicycle was arrested by a policeman for suspicious behaviour outside the Archdeacon's residence in the cathedral precincts.

When it was still an all-women college, Mrs Newman produced Benjamin Britten's *Let's Make an Opera*, in which I appeared as the cruel black-faced Sweep, and as the red-faced Coachman. This was one of my happiest experiences during my 11 years, matched only by the inspiration of special services in the cathedral, where I was an Honorary Priest Vicar, attending Evensong every day and participating in all the choral services on Sundays.

After the dedication of the new chapel, with its exterior modern sculpture and interior symbolic tapestry, the Principal decided that a suitable celebration would be a performance of Mendelssohn's oratorio, *Elijah*. I assisted Mrs Newman by conducting one of the rehearsals of the chorus, and sang the

Donald Eperson aged 9

Our wedding, left to right: Mr J.W. Eperson, Mrs A.J. Eperson, Donald, Phyllis, Rev. W.J. Perrett, Miss Bottomley (Bridesmaid), Geoffrey Perrett (Best Man), Mrs V. Perrett

Donald and Phyllis picking apples in the vicarage garden

The author at work at Bishop Otter College

Donald and Phyllis at the vicarage

Phyllis at the organ of Chilham Church

The author with, left to right: Hierlei, Vicky and Mrs Linda Cooper at Hillrise

baritone title role, whilst my friend, Mr Harvey Lansley, was the tenor soloist.

During our first year a young man taking the supplementary course in divinity began rehearsals of a Passion by Schutz with a small group of students and friends, but turned to my wife and myself for assistance, before giving a performance in chapel in which I sang the part of the Evangelist, Phyllis playing the organ accompaniment.

This led to the formation of a larger voluntary choir of students, supported by the Chaplain of the Theological College students and friends. The first work that I rehearsed and conducted was an abbreviated version of The Passion according to St John, set to music by J.S. Bach, which was accompanied by my wife at the organ. The Principal of the Theological College, Dr Moorman, attended the performance in the college chapel, and afterwards wrote to me to say he had come out of a sense of duty, but had been impressed by the quality of the singing and the prevalent reverent atmosphere. His successor, Dr Cheslyn Jones, was not so supportive, and was reported to have told his students, 'You have come here to study for Holy Orders, and not to find wives at Bishop Otter College.'

One of the few innovations that I introduced early on was the formation of a chapel council on the lines of a parochial church council, with a few ex-officio members and others elected annually by students who were regular attendants at chapel services. I can remember only one controversial issue that arose, when I was 'Dean of Chapel' and the new Chaplain, The Revd R. Shone, was Chairman. A request was made for the hymns in chapel to be sung at a lower pitch, as some young ladies found the top notes to be beyond their reach. My suggestion that as God had made sopranos and altos, as well as men tenors and basses, the complaining singers should learn the alto parts of hymns, was warmly received by Miss Murray and the rest of the council.

A far more serious problem arose about that time, when the Principal admitted to the college a young man who professed to be an atheist and said that he had been rejected by 12 state colleges of education; she hoped that living in a Christian environment would effect his conversion. Instead he created mayhem in the Chaplain's divinity lectures. One Sunday morning after the Chapel Service the Principal told me that Mr Shone would have to leave after his probationary year, as he was a failure as a divinity lecturer. I gave the Chaplain my moral support, and went with him to plead his case with the Bishop, but all in vain. The staff and the students made their farewell presentations to Mr Shone, who had been offered some unsuitable parochial posts in the diocese.

Judge of our surprise on finding at the beginning of the next term that Mr Shone was still in residence as Chaplain. He explained that during the vacation a friend had asked him what were the terms of his appointment as Chaplain; he thereupon produced a letter from the Bishop offering him the post of Chaplain for a period of five years.

So Mr Shone remained until the five years had elapsed, and then obtained a post as head of the divinity department of another college of education.

The loss of face in the eyes of staff and students suffered by the Principal by this incident had a disastrous effect upon her. She was in her mid-fifties when she became infatuated with a male student from a public school in Yorkshire, whose social graces were his main asset. He, however, preferred to spend his time in the company of a fair-haired, rosy-cheeked student who resided at the Pallant, and with other attractive maidens.

My agreement as a lecturer specified retirement at the age of 60 years, with possible extension at the discretion of the Governors to 65 years. When I asked the Principal why she would not recommend me for an extension, she replied, 'Because you have isolated yourself from your colleagues.'

When I asked, 'What makes you say that?' she said that she had come one morning into the staff common room, and seen me drinking coffee by myself in a corner of the room. I immediately left the room in silence. I met a colleague in the corridor who enquired how I had fared. I said that I had been accused of isolating myself from my colleagues. She replied, 'Well, that's a lie to begin with.'

Despite all the efforts of my friends and past students to have my appointment as mathematical lecturer extended, on the grounds that the retirement age at all other colleges of education was now 65 years, and a question being asked in Parliament on my behalf, I was forced to retire, and my wife was deprived of her post as warden and mathematical lecturer in the supplementary course for teachers.

Not a single word, spoken or written, came from the Principal or any member of the governing body to express appreciation of what my wife and I had contributed to the welfare of the college as mathematicians or as musicians. It appeared to us that Miss Murray, aided and abetted by the Archdeacon, regarded me as a menace; they were glad to have the opportunity of dismissing me, by using the obsolete clause in my agreement. Salt was rubbed into our wounds when they granted an extension to another lecturer who had reached his sixtieth birthday.

At the end of each term our voluntary choir gave a performance in the chapel of a work such as Handel's *Messiah* or his *Passion*, Vaughan Williams' *Hodie*, J.S. Bach's *St Matthew Passion*, Eric Thiman's *Last Supper*, or Bach's *St John Passion*, in a slightly abridged version, often with the assistance of a few of the lay clerks at the cathedral. Our final contributions to music in the cathedral were in 1963 and 1964, when the choral group sang the Passion according to St Luke, set to music attributed to J.S. Bach, the sole surviving copy of the score being in his handwriting.

We helped the Assistant Organist, Richard Seale, in a

performance of Britten's *St Nicolas*, and on several occasions my wife deputised for John Birch, the Cathedral organist, in accompanying Wednesday Evensongs. For some months I sang as a bass in the cathedral choir, and our contributions to the cathedral music were rewarded by the presentation by the Dean and Chapter of the two volumes of full scores of Bach's *Magnificat*.

Shortly after our arrival in Chichester the Precentor, Canon A.R. Brown Wilkinson, and I inaugurated the Thomas Weelkes Society, which rescued from oblivion, and performed at an annual Commemorative Evensong in November, some of the unpublished anthems he had composed when organist at the cathedral in Tudor times.

One of the objectives of the society was to perform the sacred and secular music that he had composed, and had been published by Stainer and Bell under the editorship of Canon E.H. Fellowes, as well as to investigate his anthems that had not been published, and were to be found in museums and libraries. I made frequent visits to the British Museum, where I soon discovered that Dr Fellowes had transcribed an anthem, *O Mortal Man*, for five voice, SAATB, but had not published it. I surmised that his reason was the unsuitability of the words, and so I compiled some alternative verses that fitted exactly the rhythm of the music. Photocopies of my manuscript of this version were made, and used by the Society. I do not know how Dr Vaughan Williams obtained a copy, but the result was that he offered to find funds to have it printed. This offer, however, never materialised, as David Willcocks (then organist at Worcester Cathedral) had it sung at an Evensong by the Three Choirs at the Gloucester Festival. Curwen's then printed my version, edited with expression marks added by the Gloucester Cathedral organist, Dr Sumsion.

David Willcocks also assisted me in reconstructing other anthems by Weelkes, but when W.S. Collins arrived in England from America with a Fulbright Scholarship in order to write a thesis on Weelkes's music, I handed over to him all the information I had acquired. During the year of residence in England he made some interesting discoveries, and when he returned to America his thesis earned a doctorate of music at one of their universities: I have always felt that I deserved half of that honour, because of my contribution. One of the facts that he unearthed was that the SATB anthem *Let Thy Merciful Ears* that Dr Fellowes had attributed to Weelkes was composed by Thomas Mudd, a contemporary organist at Peterborough Cathedral.

When the Precentor retired and then died suddenly at the age of 70, I succeeded him as president of the Chichester Music Club, which had enjoyed our recitals of Tudor motets and madrigals each term.

My wife and I also organised the Easter Singers, who were our friends who came to stay in Chichester for the Easter weekend, giving recitals of anthems in the cathedral and singing madrigals at informal concerts in the drawing room at 6 North Pallant.

The Easter Singers usually numbered about two dozen of our musical friends, several of whom we had met at the Summer School at Downe House, amongst whom was Mr Richard Bradshaw, usually known as 'Uncle Dick'.

Evensong on the Saturday evening was sung by the Easter Singers in lieu of the Cathedral Choir. On the Monday there was a recital in the cathedral in the afternoon, and a final concert in the lounge, to which we invited Canon and Mrs Lowther Clarke and a few other Chichester friends.

An enjoyable time was had by all, singing music by Morley, Weelkes, Byrd, Gibbons and their illustrious contemporary composers. Phyllis planned all the arrangements, and was responsible for the welfare of our visitors and the financial matters, whilst I had the joy of conducting a small choir of experienced singers, who shared our delight in the performance of unaccompanied music from England's Golden Age.

However, I did not expect to receive from the Bishop any expression of regret that he was losing the services of a loyal priest and his wife, who had worked together in the diocese for 11 enjoyable years.

Fortunately my reputation as a mathematician had spread far and wide, mainly because of the articles I had contributed to the *Mathematical Gazette*, describing some of my discoveries, and secondly through my contributions at conferences for mathematical lecturers. At one of these I had met Mr A.L. Flight, the Head of the Mathematical Department at the new CE College of Education at Canterbury, founded in 1962, and he secured for me a post as Senior Lecturer in Mathematics for the next five years.

9

Canterbury

In 1964 I applied for a post at Christ Church College, Canterbury, and was interviewed by the Principal, the Revd Dr F. Mason. There were two other candidates, both of whom I believe were heads of the mathematical departments at grammar schools; they withdrew their applications on learning that at a college of education the main task was to train students to teach elementary mathematics in primary and secondary school, and that there was little advanced work to be shared by the lecturers. So I became a Senior Lecturer, and joined Mr A.L. Flight, Miss Myra Gay and Mr Eddy Williamson as the fourth in a team of mathematicians. I was also able to be an honorary assistant chaplain, and to attend Evensong regularly in the cathedral, my favourite position being in the stalls behind the choir.

The college had been founded in 1962 by the Church of England, and the numbers of staff and students rose each year. I soon made friends with the head gardener – a lady who dressed like a man and smoked a pipe: she allowed me to grow pot-plants in the greenhouses on the site and in the priory garden. This activity continued for five years, and I was able to stock plant-stalls at the Christmas and summer fairs, and in the foyer at the entrance to the college, and so raise funds for the college and charitable organisations. I was also allowed to cultivate fruit and vegetables for myself in a plot of unused ground in a corner of the large garden of the Priory, which was the Principal's residence.

At the end of my first year I had a very pleasant surprise when I was elected as President of the Senior Common Room, a post I enjoyed for three consecutive years. I was the oldest member of the staff, and had had 11 years of experience in collaborating with colleagues at a college of education. A committee of members of the academic, administrative and ancillary staffs organised social events. It was my duty as President to inform the Principal of the views of SCR members whenever any major change was proposed. When the room used by the SCR was changed from a small one on the first floor to a much larger one below the dining room, my suggestion that the entrance from the cloisters should be protected by a small conservatory was accepted.

I did not relish my talks with Dr Mason, as I felt like a boy being interrogated by a stern unsmiling headmaster. The Vice-Principal, Miss I.V. Young, and Mrs Mason were much more friendly, and sometimes joined a group of madrigal singers.

At 60 years of age I became a property owner for the first time, when we bought a modernised Victorian cottage in Puckle Lane in South Canterbury, together with a garage 100 yards away in Raymond Avenue. This was to be our home for over 30 years. We paid £4000 to the builder – a Mr Mason – who had bought the dilapidated property and refurbished it, and enlarged it by an extension of the lounge and the addition of a kitchen, and a wc, bathroom and third bedroom on the first floor. It looked very attractive, with a small front garden and an American pillar rose climbing over a metal framework by the front door, but we soon discovered that appearances can be deceptive; although we had had the building surveyed, the five sash windows facing the roadway which had been retained did not operate smoothly. Next we found that Mr Mason was rather a rogue, as the dining room floorboards were decayed. When these were removed the cellar beneath was revealed, with a single vertical piece of wood supporting the horizontal beam under the floorboards. The cellar had been sealed off, so we reinstated access through a trap-door in the cupboard under the staircase, and provided ventilation into the yard. I laid a cement floor, and used the space for the storage of potatoes, apples and firewood.

The back garden was nearly a square, about 900 square feet in area, covered with builder's rubble, with a derelict apple tree at the far end, which was useful as firewood. I bought five ornamental trees to screen the surrounding commercial buildings, but only a red crab-apple tree has survived. I planted apple, pear and plum trees, red- and blackcurrant bushes and giant Himalayan blackberries. I installed a small greenhouse for growing tomatoes and pot-plants. I also maintained the gardens of three widowed neighbours for a few years and when Dr Dussart, the biology lecturer at Christ Church College, and his family, came to live at 2 Raymond Avenue, I pruned his apple trees and the sycamore hedge on the opposite side of Puckle Lane, facing our house. Later on I spent many hours in his garden, sawing up the scrapwood supplied by him and other neighbours that kept my home fire burning, together with the minimum amount of coal.

When Doreen decided to leave Shrewsbury and come to live near us in Canterbury, she bequeathed her house to the local Red Cross, hoping it would be used as flats for elderly people: this wish was not fulfilled as the property was sold, after being named Eperson House in her honour.

Doreen bought a small terraced house about ten minutes' walk away from Puckle Lane; I helped to tidy up the tiny rear garden, and used to visit her for a short time each evening and play a game of Scrabble, which she invariably won, as I was an inexperienced novice. She did not get on easily with Phyllis, and so was hardly seen at 12 Puckle Lane. When she moved to 9 Nunnery Fields, opposite St Mary Bredin's church, my main job was to clean up the cellar.

She made friends through the Red Cross and was greatly mourned when, after a few years, she was suddenly taken ill and died in Nunnery Fields Hospital. She was cremated at Barham Crematorium.

Phyllis found some temporary part-time posts teaching mathematics to sixth-form boys and girls at local grammar or technical schools, but she was busy with domestic chores every day, only allowing me to deal with the grate in the lounge, and refusing my offer to help in the kitchen with the washing-up. She sang in the Canterbury Choral Society, and in groups of madrigal singers. We both joined the Kent County Organists Association and renewed our friendship with Dr Gerald Knight, its founder. Phyllis soon served on the committee and in 1974 she was invited to be President of the KCOA; she was reluctant to accept this honour, as she disliked the idea of having to make speeches of thanks to the hosts at the conclusion of the monthly meetings of members at the parish churches and cathedrals in the county. She consented, however, on condition that I was appointed as Joint President and relieved her of any speech-making. So for the first time in its history the KCOA had a husband and wife as Joint Presidents.

The first meeting during our year of office was arranged to take place at Folkestone on a Saturday when I had already accepted an invitation to give a talk to teachers of mathematics in Leicester. Having kept this engagement, I travelled southwards in my car as quickly as I could, and reached Folkestone shortly after the meeting had ended and Phyllis had made the thank-you speech perfectly well. On subsequent occasions, and at the annual dinner, I had to make the presidential speech. I was delighted that Phyllis was honoured in this way; everyone knew that she was the expert organist, and that I was only giving her support that she did not need.

We both joined the Canterbury Music Club, and I was

invited to join the committee, the Chairman of which was Dr Alan Wicks, the cathedral organist. On his retirement I succeeded him during the 1970s; the club continued to flourish, and its membership rose to nearly 300 in the year that the Sidney Cooper Centre was reopened. Hitherto the club's recitals of chamber music by professional artistes had taken place in the halls of a number of schools and colleges in Canterbury, but the transfer of one season's recitals to the Sidney Cooper Centre proved disastrous, owing to the noise produced by other users of the building. Mr Edred Wright, the Music Director at the King's School, came to our rescue and arranged for the club to use the Shirley Hall free of charge, provided we allowed 100 boys to attend each recital. The first one in this large hall was a great success: I had invited Shura Cherkasky to be the piano soloist, and he attracted an audience of club members, about 200 of the general public and over 100 schoolboys. This was the only recital that the headmaster allowed boys to attend during the time normally devoted to preparation.

In subsequent seasons the club's membership gradually dwindled, as it served the whole of East Kent, and new music clubs were formed at the University of Kent, Whitstable and Herne Bay, which I supported by writing appreciative reports for the *Kentish Gazette* of the programmes that they presented. During my first five years in Canterbury I had occasionally sent a review of a music club recital to the *Kentish Gazette* by request, but in 1970, when the 600th anniversary of the martyrdom of St Thomas à Becket was celebrated, I was invited to become the paper's 'music critic', and review all the musical and dramatic events. I was given two tickets for each event and paid a small fee for reviews. This activity continued for over 20 years, until the editor decided that his readers were more interested in previews of future events than in reviews of past events.

Shortly after our arrival in Canterbury I enrolled as a voluntary worker at the Nunnery Fields Hospital. During the first year I was able to assist the professional gardener attached to the hospital in the maintenance of the spacious flower beds in the grounds, and when he was absent on leave for several weeks, looking after sick members of his large family, I was able to keep the beds tidy. My horticultural activities here were not altogether altruistic, as bordering the South Canterbury Road there were many old apple trees, a few pear trees and a plum tree, whose fruit was never picked, and I had the benefit of a plentiful supply of windfalls.

When Barbara Castle introduced her 'improvements' to the NHS, new plans were made for the maintenance of all hospital gardens; in East Kent a team of gardeners was centred at one hospital and spent a day working at each hospital in rotation. This resulted in my being left alone to keep the flower beds tidy at Nunnery Fields for long periods, and I was allowed to grow soft fruit on a derelict plot of ground overshadowed by the disused nurses' home.

I was licensed by Archbishop Ramsay to officiate in the diocese of Canterbury, and once had a short chat with him about his father, a Cambridge mathematician who had published books on mechanics. In subsequent years I conducted services in over 40 parish churches, and I was also a Minor Canon at the cathedral, singing Evensong at 6.30 p.m. on Sundays, when the Dean always preached and a voluntary choir led the singing to a congregation consisting mainly of students.

I resigned reluctantly from this post when the Dean and Chapter decided to close the choir school in the precincts without giving any explanation. I wrote a letter to the Dean, emphasising the value of the contribution to English music that had been made for centuries by the cathedral choir schools, and which was being continued at Salisbury and Chichester amongst other cathedrals. I received no reply or acknowledgement. Arrangements were made for the choristers and a few probationers to be educated at St Edmund's Junior

School, whilst retaining the dormitories at the disused choir school buildings in the precincts. I had known personally several of the short-lived headmasters, and a personal friend was one of the teaching staff, who all lost their jobs. It appears that the cause of this unwarranted closure was the recurrent friction between the headmasters and the governors – the Dean and Residentiary Canons of the cathedral.

My post at Christ Church College also terminated abruptly when I reached 65 years of age, and Dr Mason refused to support my plea to the governing body of the college for an extension, though the Ministry of Education had recommended that teachers and lecturers in mathematics should continue to be employed beyond 65 years of age, owing to the dearth of qualified mathematicians in the country's schools.

Mr Flight stated that I had made a 'distinctive contribution' to the mathematical department. I had conducted remedial courses for students with a dislike of mathematics, who feared the prospect of having to teach the subject in primary schools. I devised recreational mathematical activities as a remedy for 'mathephobia'. Two posts for lecturers in mathematics were advertised, but Dr Mason turned down my application for one of them ... why?

I was invited by the Headmaster of Walmer Secondary Modern School to act as 'remedial specialist' for the autumn term, whilst the music teacher was on leave. I greatly enjoyed the friendly atmosphere in the staff room, two members of which transported me daily in their cars as their homes were in Canterbury. Playing chess was the chief pastime during the break for lunch, and I devised a number of simple chess problems for the amusement of my opponents. I was even invited to adjudicate in a cake-making competition in the cookery department; fortunately, I chose as the winner the one regarded as the best by the head cook.

I enjoyed playing records of classical music once a week to a class of pupils who wanted me to play their records of pop music. I regret that I did not enjoy my mathematical activities, as I hoped that I would be in charge of the same groups of pupils each day, and show them some of the pastimes and puzzles that would enable them to discover that mathematics can be enjoyed. Instead I was sent different groups of six boys chosen by their class teachers, in the hope that I could enable them to understand the lesson given the previous day in class. At the end of that term I became an old age pensioner with a National Pension, a partial Teacher's Pension and a partial Clerical pension: however, I was not thrown on to the educational scrap-heap, but soon found employment teaching SMP mathematics to a sixth form at the King's School. A year previously I had been invited by the Headmaster to be a 'stop gap' during the illness of one of his staff, and I was permitted by Dr Mason to spend an hour each day with a sixth form class, provided that I received no salary for my services.

Later on I travelled each morning to Wye High School – a preparatory school – where for a few years I taught a class of boys and girls how to do their 'sums'. When advancing years made this a task rather than a pleasure, although the 15-mile journey through the Stour valley in summer weather was a delightful one, I resigned and was presented by the children with an album of their drawings, paintings and writings that expressed their love for me; it is one of my nicest treasures.

I also had a number of private pupils who came to me for an hour after school or at weekends; they ranged from boys about to take the Common Entrance examination, boys and girls from primary and secondary schools facing O- and A-level examinations, to two first-year university students. I can remember that most of them achieved their targets, but I can recollect the distress of one girl who failed. I visited her parents, and eventually she trained to be a nurse. From her first post at a hospital she wrote to tell me she was enjoying her work, but she was appalled by the low moral standards of some of the other residents in the nurses' home.

When the Mathematical Association began publishing its periodical *Mathematics in School*, I was invited to contribute to each issue pages of puzzles, pastimes and problems, with full solutions. This interesting activity lasted for a quarter of a century. (I still have a supply of unpublished manuscripts.) Before this I had compiled 'maths teasers' for the 'Maths Extra' issues of *The Times Educational Supplement*, and written several articles that were welcomed by the editor at that time. He chose the title 'Puzzling It Out' for the first one, in which I described my discovery of the value of 'recreational mathematics' in the classroom, based upon my experience at Sherborne School over 40 years earlier.

I continued sending occasional short 'notes' on a variety of topics to the *Mathematical Gazette*. One of these was called 'Eperson's Conjecture' – that the sum of any three consecutive square numbers (except $1^2 + 2^2 + 3^2$) could always be expressed as the sum of three other square numbers. This provoked the largest amount of correspondence ever received by the editor, from readers supplying algebraic formulae that proved that the conjecture was correct. My last conjecture in the 1990s evoked only one proof from a reader, which involved advanced mathematical reasoning that covered several pages in the *Gazette*.

Another conjecture still awaits proof. It is a corollary of Goldbach's famous unproved conjecture that every even number can be expressed as the sum of two prime numbers: 'Every even number greater than 2 can be expressed as the sum of two prime numbers in at least two ways.'

Recently I acquired a book entitled *Mathematics – The Science of Patterns*. Here the word 'science' is used as the equivalent of 'knowledge', derived from the Greek word *skio* = I know. I dislike the saying that 'Mathematics is the handmaid of science' as it degrades the realm of ideas, and implies that it is inferior to that of material things. Undoubtedly scientists today use or abuse mathematics to support their speculative theories about the material universe, but mathematics is an *art*, and not a *science*, as it is the product of human brains – a body of ideas created by intelligence, ingenuity and inspiration. Music is another form of art: it is closely associated with mathematics, as Pythagoras discovered centuries ago. There are many kinds of science, but all of them consist in investigations into the mysteries of the material Universe. Professor G.H. Hardy perceived that mathematics can be beautiful, just as a symphony by Mozart or a painting by Constable has the quality of beauty.

When I was 84 years old Blackwell's invited me to compile a book of enjoyable mathematics. The outcome was the book *Patterns in Mathematics*, which incorporated some of the material in *Mathematical Recreations*, a booklet produced with the aid of Dr Margaret Gow in 1974, which produced a profit for OXFAM of several hundreds of pounds when sold at 1s 6d a copy.

I have been unlucky in not being able to find a publisher for two other books I have written, although two different firms expressed their approval of the typescripts. One was a series of booklets, entitled *Mathematics for Pleasure*, which had been tried out in local secondary schools, and was intended as a supplement to the textbooks of utilitarian mathematics used in them. The London firm Nisbet undertook their publication, but withdrew their offer when they submitted the text to the headmasters of two London secondary modern schools, who reported that they would have no use for them in their schools. Subsequently, however, I had to supply hundreds of duplicated copies to readers of *Mathematics in School* who knew that they could use them in their classrooms to stimulate the interest of teenagers.

The other unpublished book was accepted by a new London publishing firm, which was ruined by a printer's strike and forced to cancel the publication. My book was the outcome of an investigation I had carried out in 1962 into the methods employed in training teachers to teach elementary mathematic efficiently to children in primary schools. It consisted mainly of statistics, based upon information voluntarily supplied to me by lecturers and students at over 80 of the 120-plus colleges then in operation that had assisted me in an endeavour to discover why the standard of teaching mathematics in primary schools was so poor that the Ministry of Education and the general public were shocked to find that many children left school without the ability to do simple arithmetic calculations, such as are needed in everyday life.

I despaired of looking for another commercial publisher, and did not consider publishing it at my own expense, or writing an article summarising the facts – that several training colleges had no mathematician or their staff, and others had no schemes for elementary mathematical training or for testing the ability to teach arithmetic on final school practice.

CHILHAM

The first time I had visited Chilham was in 1928 when on a cycle tour with my father in south-east England, as I have mentioned. Some 40 years later Phyllis and I were for several years closely associated with the residents in this village, making many friends, including a retired doctor and his wife who were not churchgoers. For several weeks I acted as *locum tenens* during a vacancy, and Phyllis was the organist. The events in the following years are described briefly in my booklet, *Reminiscences of Barchester*, but as a full account would take up many pages in this autobiography, I will record only the final event. In the *Chilham Parish Magazine* for August 1983 Mr Colthop, the Senior Churchwarden and Honorary Treasurer of the PCC, wrote:

Now that Mrs Eperson is no longer our organist, some

tribute should be made to the splendid service she has given us over the past seventeen years. Mrs Eperson first came to Chilham to play the organ in a part-time capacity in Canon Lawson's time, and with the arrival of the next Vicar she was engaged on a permanent basis.

She has given faithful service to our Parish Church for a number of years at a fee which by modern standards was very small, and we are pleased to record our thanks and appreciation for the part she has played in assisting with our church worship.

Canon Eperson has also become a familiar figure to our congregation, and we look back with gratitude to the many occasions when he has taken our services and given us some forthright addresses.

It is with the greatest regret we learn that he will no longer be joining in our services. He has been a kind and generous friend to Chilham.

The local correspondent of the *Kentish Gazette* published her own version of the story of my wife's forced resignation, when a new vicar exercised his legal right 'to hire and fire the organist', who had committed no offence. Shortly afterwards Canon Dawson resigned, as he found life in a rural parish intolerable, and was provided with a non-parochial post as Diocesan Missioner.

Amongst our friends in Chilham were a retired Church of England priest and his wife, who owned some property in France, which they visited from time to time, and returned with the bottled product of its vineyard and other choice wines. We continued to enjoy the sumptuous suppers to which they invited us occasionally until they left Chilham.

Sadly Phyllis broke her left leg twice through falls in her kitchen shortly after leaving Chilham, thus terminating a brilliant career as an organist. As soon as she left the hospital, she returned on Sundays to play the piano at the Holy Communion Services in the chapel, and I assisted the Chaplain, whom we knew when he was a student at Chichester Theological College and a singer in a choral group at Bishop Otter College; he was now a Canon.

We soon became friends with Mrs Evelyn Anderrson, the sacristan, her daughter and son-in-law, Bridget and Rodney Britton, and Alf T. Fisher, who kindly transported us in his car to and from the hospital. The next Chaplain was the Revd Helen Connell, though by now I could assist only by reading the Gospel. Although permanently walking with crutches, Phyllis was a lively, strong and healthy old lady in her eighties. Until I was in my 94th year I continued to drive our car, using it mainly for our touring holidays, and to attend concerts in and around Canterbury. I often travelled 300 miles in a day, my longest trip being to reach Moffat in the Scottish Lowlands by 8 p.m.

By the 1990s, driving a car had become more of a task than a pleasure, owing to traffic congestion in built-up areas and increasing heavy vehicles on motorways, so I decided not to renew my driving licence. Physical activities brought on breathlessness, but I continued at the Nunnery Fields Hospital, sawing up firewood and making a daily shopping trip, collecting our pensions from the post office in Oaten Hill (and taking them to deposit at a building society) and growing cuttings of flowering shrubs for sale at OXFAM.

I had two operations for removal of cataracts, and had a short spell in hospital after knocking myself unconscious on a wall when avoiding an oncoming motorcyclist, and occasionally after nasal haemorrhages due to high blood pressure. Otherwise old age was pleasant for both of us, until 1997, when Phyllis fell in our lounge, badly damaging her head against a hard piece of furniture. I continued with my domestic chores and cookery, but by the end of a week I too was in hospital after a bad nose-bleed.

Neither of us was fit to return home, and we went to live at a nearby nursing home in the Old Dover Road. High Meadow accommodated about 40 residents, most of whom sat silently in chairs in a large lounge. We had a pleasant bed-sitting room on the ground floor, which opened on to a well-kept garden, and had our meals with the other residents. We were well looked after but found only one person able and willing to converse with us – a former employee in the kitchen at Christ Church College. A few weeks after our arrival Phyllis had a hysterectomy, from which she made a remarkably quick recovery, and felt fit enough to return home. I agreed to this on condition that we had regular domestic help, because I had been becoming exhausted by the daily expeditions to shops less than a mile away, as I had to rest several times on the return journey, carrying bags of food and drink. Phyllis concurred, and accordingly I contacted an agency and arranged to have assistance for one hour each weekday. After the first week we could consider whether to increase the amount of help, if desirable. By this time Phyllis had followed her mother's example in old age and become increasingly forgetful – not only mislaying things in the house, but also failing to remember decisions we had made together. So we left the nursing home and returned to No. 12 Puckle Lane. At the end of the first day I suggested that I should phone the agency, and ask for a helper to come on the next day; but Phyllis had forgotten about the agreement, and replied, 'No woman is ever going to come into my kitchen.' I carried on as before as best as I could, but after a few days I was completely exhausted. We were forced to leave home a second time.

On the recommendation of our solicitor, Mr Andrews, we moved to the Old Rectory, a residential home for the elderly not far from Canterbury. We had a fine large bed-sitting room on the first floor in the oldest part of the building, reputed to have been erected in the thirteenth century. We furnished it with our own beds, wardrobes, bookcases, desk and old oak chest, and hung a number of our pictures on the walls; everything was fumigated on arrival. There was a beautiful large garden and a full-time professional gardener in residence to look after some greenhouses. Each Sunday morning we were taken by car to attend a Holy Communion service in a nearby village church, usually Littlebourne.

I was able to settle down there and pursue my normal activities, although there were very few other residents who were able and willing to talk to us in the lounge. Phyllis was not so contented as I was, as she did not relish the excellent food, produced by a professional chef and assistant cooks. Eventually she was provided with a simple diet that suited her. Phyllis was also irritated by the young women nurses who bathed both men and women residents.

The Matron, Kim, asked me to perform an arithmetic calculation on her computer, as she wished to distribute a legacy for her staff in proportion to the total number of hours of service they had given. She also allowed me to use the computer to produce copies of a circular letter to our friends.

Once a week some form of entertainment was provided for residents, and so I volunteered to give an illustrated talk on Lewis Carroll. Kim had my film-strip 'Alice in Numberland' cut up and made into slides. I was greatly shocked when in the absence of Kim, the secretary cancelled the talk at the last moment, because she said she could not operate the projector, and arranged for another resident to take my place. This affected my health for a few weeks. I did not renew my offer, but told Kim that I could give a talk and a display of some of Carroll's well-known books and other publications, including the modern edition of his diaries, from which most of my information about his life and activities had been taken. This proved to be so much appreciated that a few weeks later I gave a second talk – on 'Lewis Carroll Mathematician'. I used a felt pen and a white 'blackboard' to show some of the numerical and word puzzles that he had compiled for the amusement of his young friends. At Christmastide I won the prize in a quiz competition; it was a radio set, which I donated to the home, as we had a very good radio of our own.

10

Worthing

Some years previously Phyllis and I discussed possible plans for the time when old age would make it impossible to remain in our home. I made enquiries about the Church of England's retirement homes for clergy and their wives, and received information about one in Surrey which also had a nursing home for residents who became ill. In the autumn of 1997 we were notified by the CE Pensions Board that some old buildings in Worthing were being refurbished and would shortly be opened as Ramsay Hall. The prospect of living in Worthing with congenial companions was very attractive to us, as we knew the town well.

When my wife's parents, Canon and Mrs W.J. Perrett, retired from Shipley, Yorkshire, they bought a house in Ripley Road, West Worthing, and we were able to travel from Chichester on Sunday evenings, and go with them to Evensong in churches nearby, such as Goring, where I was once invited to preach. This ended when we moved to Canterbury in 1964, and shortly afterwards they followed us, and bought a house in Norman Road, about five minutes' walk away.

So in 1997 we obtained information about the financial conditions and regulations for residents at Ramsay Hall, and applied for a flat, sending a certificate from our NHS doctor in Canterbury, Dr Jones, stating that we were suitable as residents at a retirement home, as we had been for some months at the Old Rectory. In reply we were invited to visit Ramsay

Hall and meet the prospective warden, Mrs James, who was then in charge of a similar retirement home in the Midlands.

We travelled by taxi to Worthing one afternoon, and spent over a pleasant hour in the chapel. Phyllis conversed with Mrs James about domestic matters, whilst her husband drew sketches for me, showing the dimensions of the floors and windows of a flat, as we had to provide carpets and curtains as well as all the furniture. We returned to the Old Rectory feeling pleased at the prospect of greater independence in a home with congenial fellow residents with similar backgrounds. A few days later we gladly accepted the offer of a flat by the Pensions Board, and wrote agreeing to the conditions. I drew plans to show how our furniture could be fitted into the rooms of our flat, and paid over £800 for new carpets to cover the floor. It cost £1,000 to transport our property from the Old Rectory and the lounge and dining room furniture from 12 Puckle Lane to Worthing. On Wednesday, January 21st, 1998, we were given a cheerful send-off from the Old Rectory by Kim and the staff, and travelled by taxi to Worthing.

The Pensions Board has supplied me with some of the following information about events after our arrival at Ramsay Hall.

We were warmly greeted by the warden and handed the keys of our flat about 3.30 p.m. She told us that the parcel of curtains that we had sent by post some ten days previously was so badly damaged that they could not be hung in our rooms, but she did not produce them for us to see whether they could be repaired. I handed her a letter from my district nurse in Canterbury, addressed to the district nurse in Worthing who would take over responsibility for our care, informing her of the occasional treatment that I had had. The warden opened this letter, and having read the message (which she probably did not understand), she promptly phoned the Pensions Board in London to express her 'grave doubts' as to whether my medical needs could be met at Ramsay Hall. There is no record of the reply – it was probably advice to consult the NHS doctor attached to Ramsay Hall.

When the furniture van arrived about 5 o'clock the men began unloading a number of cardboard boxes containing books, papers, correspondence and pictures, but when the warden noticed that a small wooden box containing silver cutlery had been affected by woodworm, she jumped to the conclusion that the rest of our furniture might be infected, and she refused to allow the men to unload any more, and ordered the men to take the remainder back to our house in Canterbury, where it was all dumped in the ground floor rooms. This was a serious mistake, because our bedroom furniture had been fumigated on arrival at the Old Rectory. Later our mahogany dining room furniture and an old grandfather clock were illustrated in the auctioneers' sale catalogue, and fetched a very good price. Our lounge and bedroom furniture and the carpets could not be sold legally, and were destroyed, together with the contents of the kitchen cupboards. I estimate their value at over £2,000.

We enjoyed our supper with the other residents, and spent the evening in their company. The warden allowed us to sleep in a guest room, and we joined the other residents for breakfast. About 10 a.m. we were interviewed by Dr Sandon, the home's NHS consultant. He did not examine me, but simply stated that I was 'in need of continuous nursing care' and therefore unsuitable for Ramsay Hall. After leaving the room in silence, the warden immediately told us that she knew of a nearby nursing home. When we asked when we could see the nursing home, we were told that the doctor knew of a better one, which we assumed was in Worthing, as we had told the warden that we would like to be near Ramsay Hall, so that we could enjoy its amenities, and Phyllis would be able to accompany the hymns at services in the chapel. After lunch, however, we were taken by Mr and Mrs James in their car, with a few of our cardboard boxes in the boot, to Sandena, a large nursing home at Findon, about 7 miles north of Worthing, nestling in a valley in the South Downs near Cissbury Ring. There were only a few other residents, whom we seldom met, as we had all our meals in our room on the ground floor. The Matron did her best to enable us to feel 'at home', but our unjustified ejection from Ramsay Hall had a devastating effect upon Phyllis, destroying her expectation of a peaceful old age. The other cardboard boxes soon arrived and were stored in a garage, but I immediately recovered my typewriter and writing paper, and sent a letter to our solicitor in Canterbury, telling him about our plight, and asking him to send a complaint about our treatment at Ramsay Hall to the CE Pensions Board in London.

When we were visited by the Vicar of Findon, and the local representative of the Retired Clergy Association, Canon Christopher Blair-Fish, and by friends living in Steyning and Bognor Regis, Phyllis would complain bitterly to them about her treatment; she felt like a prisoner, far from the sea and shops of Worthing, unable even to take a stroll because the surrounding lanes were steep and dangerously narrow for pedestrians. Soon we were transferred to a bed-sitting room on the first floor, and I was allowed to use a small adjoining room as my 'office', with a desk and some of my cardboard boxes, and so I was able to continue with some of my normal activities. But Phyllis could only sit all day moaning and groaning, sometimes exclaiming, 'That wicked doctor ought to be punished.' Often at night time she would become hysterical, and two night nurses would try to calm her, but it could take over an hour before she settled down to sleep.

The Vicar of Findon and some of his parishioners were kind and helpful, transporting us each Sunday to the 11 o'clock Service of Holy Communion at Findon church, or to Sutton church, which we reached along the beautiful valley road known as the Long Furlong. I recollected that I had first visited Findon when on my first long cycle ride of about 50 miles with my father: we rode from East Acton along the main road from London to Worthing, and branched off at Findon along the Long Furlong to Littlehampton.

I shared my wife's bitter disappointment, but felt I could do nothing to improve our lot. Canon Blair-Fish found a solution that would end our misery, as he knew of a private retirement home in Worthing, which he invited us to visit.

We met Mrs Linda Cooper, SRN, in a large ground-floor sitting room at Hillrise, 12 Tennyson Road, that was soon to be our home for the rest of our days. We moved in on March 30th, 1998, and our cardboard boxes were stored in the cellar. The next problem was to recover my oak desk, old oak chest (a family heirloom) and other items from our Canterbury home. Transport of the furniture by a Canterbury carrier cost £100, but we had to be taken by car to Canterbury by a local second-hand dealer in order to find the special shoes that Phyllis needed, and a few small oddments, in return for which he took some of our belongings, worth at least £50. Our remaining goods and chattels were left behind for the 'clearers'; these included a new gas cooker, a refrigerator, a new large storage cupboard, a larder full of tinned and bottled food – mostly fruit from our garden – a spin-drier, and a cupboard full of crockery. Their total value would probably be several thousands of pounds.

I had been content at Sandena, where we were registered with Dr Patel, who tried unsuccessfully to change my medication, but Phyllis was glad to be released from her 'prison'. We could walk on Sundays to Holy Trinity church, and on weekdays to the sea front in warm weather. I hoped that the change would restore Phyllis's equanimity, but this was not to happen, as her mental health gradually deteriorated, despite the skilful care of the staff at Hillrise.

Within a year her mental health had deteriorated so much that she sometimes remarked that I was not her husband but a make-believe imposter. Nevertheless she allowed me each evening to show her the kind of affection a husband has for a beloved wife. By 1999 she needed continuous nursing care. She could no longer look after herself as regards dressing and washing, and resented the attentions of the carers.

One evening, a new young night-carer arrived, and I could hear my poor demented wife resisting her efforts to make her comfortable for the night. The next morning I told Linda that I feared the inexperienced newcomer would be so disgusted by the rough treatment she had received from one she was trying to help that she would give up such unrewarding work. Linda told me that Vicky, a student from Georgia with a strong character, would not easily give in. So for several weeks I endured hearing my poor wife responding to kindness with hostility.

Before long Phyllis became so confused that she abandoned the use of the crutches she had used for over ten years, after having two falls in her kitchen that resulted in fractures above and below the knee of her left leg. She tried to totter round the house, and despite frequent warnings the inevitable result was a fatal fall, gashing her head and damaging her weak left leg. She was taken to Southlands Hospital, Shoreham, where Linda kindly took me to visit her during the next fortnight. Linda realised that she would not survive much longer, as Phyllis was conscious but speechless, and she persuaded the authorities to allow Phyllis to return to Hillrise by ambulance. Linda and I were by her bedside day and night for a fortnight, until she passed away peacefully at 9 p.m. on May 4th 2000.

A Thanksgiving Service for her life at Holy Trinity Church was attended by many friends. I read some Tudor love-lyrics that had been set to music as madrigals, and Linda read the poem *What is our life?* written by Sir Walter Raleigh on the eve of his execution. The organist played music from the repertory of pieces that Phyllis loved, and the funeral service was followed by burial in the beautiful cemetery at the entrance to the Findon valley. On the coffin lay a sheaf of lilies, similar to the one she had carried at our wedding 61 years earlier. Friends were asked not to send floral tributes, but were invited to give donations to the British Red Cross, which benefited by about £400. Refreshments were provided by Linda at Hillrise to the friends who had travelled a long way. I was very pleased to see James Gillespie, who had succeeded me as leader of the group of madrigal singers that for several years had met regularly at Poulton Manor, Ash, Kent, the home of Lord and Lady Arbuthnot, to whom I am indebted for their many kindnesses.

Now that I was a widower the sole duty of the night-nurse was to bring me a cup of Horlicks at 10 p.m., and some of them would stay for a few minutes' chat. Most of all I enjoyed conversations with Vicky, who could speak five languages and was training to be a tourist guide. We had interesting discussions, such as the differences between the Classical Greek that I learnt at school and the modern Greek language. I enjoyed her short visits so much that a platonic friendship gradually developed between us, with the approval of Linda. I endeavoured to increase her vocabulary of the English language, and gave her some 'homework' to do each week. Before she left England for a nine-week summer vacation, Vicky told me that I had helped her, and I said that I had enjoyed having conversations of an intellectual kind. When we had discussed the fact that five different Greek words in the original text of the New Testament were translated in the Authorised Version of the Bible by the single word 'love', we came to the conclusion that Christian love meant the desire to make life happy for others, or to alleviate their suffering. So the most important activity in human life was to show Christian love towards everyone possible.

Linda and her staff were wonderfully kind to me during my bereavement, especially on my 96th birthday, when each of them sent me a birthday card and some made me a present. I was overwhelmed with gratitude when a card and present from the absent Vicky were given to me; she had left them behind for me before she left England.

Vicky also listened sympathetically to me as I 'walked through the valley of the shadow of death', grieving over the loss of a wife who had been lovable, loving and lovely throughout the first 59 years of married bliss. The only time we were separated was when she returned for a few weeks to her parents' home in Shipley, so that she could go to the Bradford Royal Infirmary. Before we were married she was suffering from sciatica, the cause of which was never diagnosed by the surgeons at the Dorchester County Hospital. At Bradford it was immediately seen that the cause was a 'slipped disc', visible to the naked eye. After treatment she returned to Charminster, and was never troubled again.

When I no longer had her company I became depressed, thinking I should never feel happy again, but Vicky cured me of my melancholia. Her smiling face and slim figure were a pleasure to see, but it was what she said to me that inspired me to realise that life was still worth living, as I could continue to show Christian love towards others.

My friends living outside Worthing also gave me valuable support; Joyce Honer from Steyning and Mary Gostling from Bognor Regis visited me frequently, and I maintained correspondence with Dr Harry Higginson and Dr Georges Dussart in Canterbury; the latter has visited me twice, and is able to keep my old typewriter in working condition, so that I can continue writing articles on a variety of topics, ranging from Lewis Carroll to recreational mathematics, for publication at home and abroad.

When Vicky returned to England to complete her course of study, she brought the good news that she was engaged to be married in July 2001, and that she had changed her mind about her vocation, having met a friend who was working with deprived children under the Red Cross. She has the right temperament and motivation for such work; moreover, she will be living near her parents, instead of wandering around the world talking to strangers.

Vicky comes twice a week to Hillrise, and her ministrations as night-nurse are appreciated by residents and staff alike. At present (March 2001) Monica is the only resident with whom I can exchange a few words at meal times, and she is full of praise for Vicky's conscientious care for the other residents who need her attention for a longer time when getting to bed. Vicky arrives at 8 p.m. and is kept busy until after midnight, when 'Smoky Joe' decides he has had enough TV watching. Usually Vicky is able to spend only a short time with me, sometimes reading passages from a modern English translation of the New Testament, and I need no assistance in getting to bed before midnight. She has told me that she 'almost regards me as one of her family' – a deputy grandfather.

Vicky and Linda are now my two best friends upon earth. Almost every day Linda shows me an extra kindness, such as discussing my problem about Ramsay Hall and making suggestions about the next step to be taken in my prolonged controversy with the CE Pensions Board. In January 1998 my Canterbury solicitor complained to the board about our unjustifiable ejection from Ramsay Hall within 24 hours of arrival and being handed the keys of our flat. A reply was sent by an official at the London headquarters, expressing regret but stating that the board had no responsibility for the conduct of its employees at its residential homes. The result of the exchange of many letters was that we were refunded the £800+ we had spent on fitting new carpets to the rooms of our flat.

Fortunately I can finish this story of my life so far on a happy note: I have been able to express my gratitude to Linda for her many kindnesses by helping her to solve the problem of the future education of her son Oliver, who is now at a preparatory school in Worthing. In due course he will be a boarder at Sherborne School, after being interviewed by the Headmaster and by his future housemaster.